Early Years Foundation Stage Profile
Exemplification Materials

<Ordered into the 17 EYFS Early Learning Goals>

To purchase a copy please visit:

www.thenationalcurriculum.com

or scan this code to take you there:

© Crown copyright 2013
Corporate Author: The Department For Education
Published by: Shurville Publishing

The materials in this book are also available to download from www.education.gov.uk

Contents

Exemplification of expected descriptors

This document demonstrates national standards for [the] 17 Early Years Foundation Stage (EYFS) Profile Early Learning Goals (ELGs). It shows the level of learning and development expected at the end of the EYFS.

The collection of evidence in this document illustrates the 'expected' descriptor. No one piece of evidence meets the ELG as a standalone item; together they illustrate the pitch and breadth of a particular 'expected' level of learning and development.

This document illustrates how information can be gathered to support EYFS Profile judgements using a variety of evidence and forms of presentation. However there is no prescribed method of gathering evidence, nor any expectation that it should be recorded as shown in this document. The exemplification is not intended to be an exhaustive list for schools to follow.

The examples in this collection include 'one off' observations, samples of children's work, photographs and contributions from parents. Many methods of recording a child's attainment are not included in this exemplification for practical reasons (for example video recordings). Practitioners will also build up a significant professional knowledge of each child which will not be recorded but which must be considered when EYFS Profile judgements are made.

When completing an EYFS Profile, practitioners should make a best-fit judgement for each ELG. Practitioners must consider the entirety of each ELG, taking an holistic view of the descriptor in order to create the most accurate picture of the child's overall embedded learning. Sections of each descriptor must not been seen in isolation.

Exemplification material should always be viewed in the context of a specific aspect of learning in order to retain an accurate focus. However, practitioners should be aware that a child's learning and development are not compartmentalised. Focussing on one aspect of learning will shed light on several other related areas.

The information in this document should not be regarded as either exclusive or inclusive of any child, no matter what their background or family circumstances. It is intended to be used without bias, preference or discrimination and schools and practitioners must ensure that they operate within all aspects of the statutory EYFS framework.

EYFS Profile exemplification for the level of learning and development expected at the end of the EYFS

Communication and language

ELG01 – Listening and attention

> **Children listen attentively in a range of situations. They listen to stories, accurately anticipating key events and respond to what they hear with relevant comments, questions or actions. They give their attention to what others say and respond appropriately, while engaged in another activity.**

Context
Emily is sat in a small group listening to a story.

Observation
' I know what happens next! Goldilocks goes upstairs and sleeps in baby bears bed. Then the bears come home. I think she was scared'

Context – Parental observation
Amber is listening to some music with me in the lounge

Observation

We were listening to classical music and Amber was picking out all the instruments she could hear and telling us which ones she could hear. She was also doing different dances depending on the music and saying what the music reminded her of 'its like fairies' or ' a spooky forest'

Context
Tom is recalling the adventures of the 'Adventure bear' as he travels around the world

Observation

'He starts in England, then goes to Australia, then into the sea and then into Canada and then he goes into............what other countries have cold weather? '

Another child says Africa

'No its too hot there ....well he can go back to Australia'

Matthew was playing outside in the role play area that had been turned into a birthday cake bakery. He rolled a sausage shape with play-dough and began slicing it into circles. Claire drove up on a delivery bike and asked: "Are you making cakes?" Matthew looked up: "No I'm making little breads". He continued cutting... "No actually, I'm making cherries".

After listening to the story of "Goldilocks and the Three Bears", Matthew chose to work at the sand tray. As he made sandcastles he chatted to the other children who were making different shapes in the sand. "I've made a big sandcastle, a little sandcastle and a middle sized one!" he said.*

Matthew listened hard to the story of "The Three Little Pigs", When asked: "Which houses will blow down?" He explained: "The straw house because the straw isn't strong enough".

S chose to paint a picture of an ostrich. "I like ostriches there is one in our story 'Handa's surprise'. The body needs to be brown and black. It has pink legs". While she painted she chatted about the ostrich taking the fruit in the story. "I'm going to paint some background – sky and grass".*

When listening to Handa's surprise Elouise said 'I bet that goat is going to knock Handa's basket off'

Early Years Unit

Name :   Freddie

Date:

No. of terms spent in EY Unit: 1 Language English	**Information on the activity** Adult directed/Child initiated Interaction: individually/**pair**/group/ Time of day: **am**/pm Area/Location: Role play

OBSERVATION

Freddie was working alongside his friends in the 3 Bears cottage and was setting the table ready for lunch. He was encouraged to sort the cups, bowls and spoons into the 3 sizes (small, medium and large). He confidently matched up each place setting and spoke clearly about what he was doing. "Daddy bear needs the BIG spoon and Daddy bear needs to sit on the BIG chair. That's not his chair, that's the medium-sized chair for mummy bear." He swapped the chairs over. "That's better!" he said. He then went onto finding the place setting for mummy bear. "Where is the medium-sized bowl?" said Freddie looking in the cupboards. "Found it!" he called out. As he was setting baby bears place at the table the practitioner imitated the sound of the phone ringing. Freddie ran to the phone. "I bet it's Goldilocks.............yes it is! You have been very naughty and ate all baby bears porridge and broke his chair. You can't come and play at my house", he shouted slamming down the phone. Freddie pretended the phone was ringing again. "Oh no! It's Goldilocks again. What now? You can't come and eat all our food. We are going to lock the doors." At this point the practitioner intervened saying, "If she promises to play nicely and be good, can she come and play?"
"Okay then." Freddie replied. She can come in 10 minutes. I will count to 10 and wait for her. 1, 2, 3, 4............." Freddie counted orally to 10 carefully and confidently. He continued to play alongside his friends getting lunch ready for Goldilocks. After about 30 minutes of sustained play he followed his friends outside.

Page 6   Page 6

Ben in cave

"We are going under the blankets to read a story, it is dark under there so we can use our torches. It is like being in a cave, really dark."

Ben, talking about safety with cables etc.

"You mustn't touch cause you will be electrocuted and then you might even die."

Listened to traditional tale of 3 little pigs and transfers this to independent play using three little pig puppets.

Ben + Kenzie
3 little pigs puppets.
Ben - W

I am going to blow your house down, now um going down the chimney and this is the chimney (Put a block on others) "here I come" oh no arghh! " Wolf burnt his bottom!!

"Little pig, little pig let me come in and um blow your house in "

Whilst taking down patient information in role as a doctors receptionist Jessica turned round to listen to Scarlet about another patient being brought into the surgery. She then returned to her notebook to continue writing down the patients name and symptoms.

J's favourite child choice activity is school teacher role play!

She had chosen this story from the book box and handled it as though sharing it with the class.

Good book handling skills – tracking text from left to right.

Looking closely at the pictures – identifying characters and the sequence of the story, J became aware of S. "Are you listening to my story? ...the end!"

EYFS Profile exemplification for the level of learning and development expected at the end of the EYFS

Communication and language

ELG02 – Understanding

> **Children follow instructions involving several ideas or actions. They answer 'how' and 'why' questions about their experiences and in response to stories or events.**

Matthew and Claire chose to play in the three pigs' cottage. M knocked on the window and said "Let me in, let me in!". C replied "No! No! Not by the hairs on my chinny chin chin!" M shouted "Then I'll huff and I'll puff and I'll huff!". C: "Well you can't blow it down cos our home is made of bricks!"

Matthew was playing outside with the crates, bamboo guttering and cars. Some materials had been added to the provision. He explained what would happen if different materials were put onto the ramp: "If I put fabric down the ramp, what will happen to the car?" "It will go slow because it will get in the way of the wheels".

Matthew was experimenting with different materials in the water tray investigating which would make the best hat to keep Mrs. Honey dry. He was able to find a suitable material and explain why it would be better than others. When asked "Why are the paper and the cloth not good?" he explained, "if the water goes through it's not good for the hat; it's not waterproof. On the plastic bag one it didn't go through so it is waterproof".

Context
A treasure hunt was set up by the teacher in the outside area reading clues using positional language and key words to follow the trail to find Bertie bears hiding place.

Observation

Maria
'It says .....look in the box.....n.e.x.t. next to the tap'
Come on its over there..........

She continued to follow the written clues using her phonic knowledge to sound out common unfamiliar words until she found Bertie... under the sand pit.

The game had been introduced the previous week, Luke chose this game and enjoyed playing an addition game on the Smartboard today. He had to recognise the number on the card and then find two dice from a choice of five that added together to make that number. Luke correctly found two dice to add together for all of these number cards!

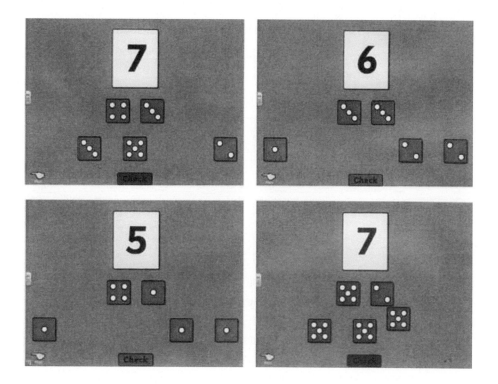

As I was driving to school this morning, Luke and Matilda began talking to each other about how old they are. Matilda said, "Luke, I'm 6 years old!" After arguing back and forth about this for a while Luke said to me, "She's not 6 is she mum, because she is younger than me and I'm only 5. Matilda is only 2 isn't she mum?"

Luke then went on to explain to Matilda, "when you're 6, I'll be 7, because I'm older than you."

On hearing this I said to Luke, "if Matilda is 2 and you are 5, how many years older are you?"

Luke was able to work it out and answered "3". So I then asked, "so if you are 3 years older than Matilda, when Matilda is 6 how old will you be?"

Luke thought for a while, then answered, "I'll be 9 then won't I mum!"

Tiger mask

'Grrr' said Lois. 'Do you want me to help you Jessica?' Lois had successfully completed her tiger mask using different media and materials. The children had been inspired by story of The Tiger Who Came To Tea and chose to make masks in response to the story. When asked why Lois's Tiger looked sad she replied – 'He's hungry that's why he has come to tea!

Evidence	
1. The Magic Wand	Grace had returned to school after the weekend eager to show the class her work and tell the teacher about her magic wand. Grace wanted to use the 'wand' to become a spider so that she could creep up on Ellie her sister. The teacher asked Grace 'Why do you want to turn into a spider and creep up on Ellie? Grace replied 'Because she is always jumping out on me and she is scared of spiders!'
2. The hungry caterpillar	In an independent activity Ruby sequenced the story with another child. She was keen to show the teacher and responded to questions about the story. 'I would feel sick like the caterpillar if I ate all that food!'

Context
Following the story 'Olivers milkshake' the children were making milkshakes for snack. Adam had listened to the instructions about how to record his favourite. Resources were set up in the 'café' area.

Observation

Adam tasted all the milkshakes and then he chose a piece of brown paper to show he liked chocolate best.

He wrote his name ' A.d.a.m' on the paper and said 'That's 'cos I like chocolate best'

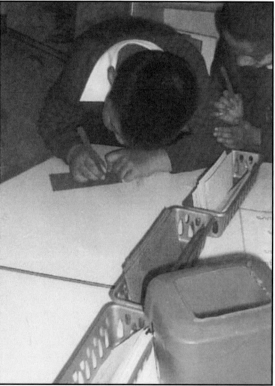

Evidence towards
<u>Listening and attention</u>
Listens and responds
Give attention
Relevant comments

Links to
PD - M

Learning Characteristics	
By playing and exploring	He tasted all the milkshakes to find out which he liked best. He wasn't too keen to try the strawberry at first.
Through active learning	Very focused on completing the task.
Creating and thinking critically	

EYFS Profile exemplification for the level of learning and development expected at the end of the EYFS

Communication and language

ELG03 – Speaking

Children express themselves effectively, showing awareness of listeners' needs. They use past, present and future forms accurately when talking about events that have happened or are to happen in the future. They develop their own narratives and explanations by connecting ideas or events.

Sketch – experimenting with instruments.

Coby talked as he experimented.

Rainstick -shaking at first then tipping.

"Mmm, this is interesting. It's from Chinese I think. It sounds like balls, tiny balls. It's rain and…….. and like thunder."

Cabassa- Shaking at first then asking a practitioners- "How does this work?"

"It sounds like scraping."

"It's really hard."

Giving to peer- "Can you do that? Try then! I'll hold it and you do it!"

Shaker- "This one's like snow! Remember when it snowed a bit ago. It was brilliant! We made a snowman he was even taller than me."

Coby continued to work with the instrument playing a complex and repeat rhythm of short and long sounds.

Sketch

Lyla worked with a group making natural sculptures in response to looking at the work of Andy Goldsworthy.

She talked the activity through as she worked, "That looks a bit like a spiral.....this feels rough!"" .... Look!.. The sun!"

When she had finished she explained what she had learnt, "I learnt about resources, wooden resources, leaves, curled up leaves. I liked putting the resources in different places to make it how I wanted to!" She added thoughtfully, "I learnt how to dream about stones and rocks and leaves."

When she had finished she said proudly, "I want everyone to see it!"

She took this photo of her work. "I can take photos. I know how to 'cos Miss Ford told me yesterday. I'm going to do it again when I make something special."

Context

Sam is in the role play area – the vets surgery

Observation

Sam has taken the dog and written an appointment on the appointment sheet. He rewrites the appointment on an appointment card and fills in some Pet details giving them both to me.

'I am going to operate on the dog. He's broken all his body, a policeman…no a robber jumped all over him when he had broken into a house. I can mend him though……come back for him in 5 days

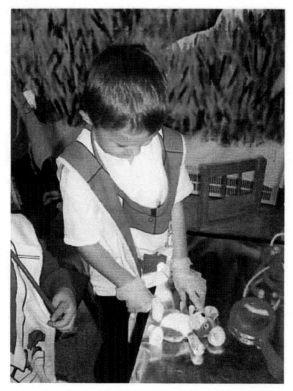

Pet Details

My pet's name: _____

Type of animal: _____

Symptoms:

Treatment:

Signed:_____ Date:_____

Appointments

Time	Name
8:00am	
9:00am	
10:00am	
11:00am	
12:00pm	
1:00pm	
2:00pm	
3:00pm	
4:00pm	
5:00pm	

Context

Anoop and Amy are in the café role play area

Observation

Anoop – 'What would you like to eat?'
Amy – 'Cake'
Anoop – 'Actually we don't have cake'
Amy – 'Don't you have any cake?'
Anoop shrugged and shook his head
Adult – 'Whats happened to the cake?
Anoop – 'Ermm. Some people stole them so we just have ice cream, hot dogs, eggs, melon and grapes'
Amy – 'grapes'
Anoop – 'O.K coming right up. Grapes……..here you go'

Context

Sam had spent 10 minutes building a construction with the wooden blocks.

Observation

'This is my road for my car. There is water down there so you have to go really slowly at the side of the road so as not to fall over the side. My dad drives slowly near the water'

Context
Sasha comes over to Lily who is in the mark making area.

Observation

'Lily I cant come to your party because I am going to my other friends house after school and then to swimming lessons and ballet lessons'

Matthew played with the small world characters with Jacob and they took it in turns to retell the story of 'Goldilocks and the Three Bears'.

M: "*Mummy bear made some porridge and she gived it to daddy bear and she gived it to baby bear and then they said 'it's too hot'. And mummy bear and daddy bear and baby bear went for a walk*".

J: "*Then Goldilocks came. She ate… First she tried daddy bear's porridge and it was too salty then she tried mummy bear's and it was too sweet then she tried baby bear's and it was just perfect!*"

M: "*Then she tried the seats and she tried daddy bear's one but it was too hard and she tried mummy bears one and it was too soft and she tried baby bears one and it had a pillow on it and it was just right! And she broke it! And then she went up to the stairs and went to try daddy bear's bed and it was too hard and she tried mummy bears but it was too soft and she tried baby bear's one and it was just right! She fell asleep and the bears came back and she ran away.*"
(Transcript of tape recording using easi-speak microphone).

They enjoyed listening to their story re-play afterwards.

At the water tray Matthew dropped different objects into the water and guessed if the objects would float. "I think the apple will sink because it's fat. I think the brick will sink because it's heavy. I think it (plastic lid) will float because it isn't that heavy" .

The group had been studying nocturnal animals and looking at factual books. Zak showed a growing understanding of the natural world when working in clay. He explained, "I like bats because they fly and because they eat flies. They wake up at night because they want to play with the animals. Bats! They sleep all through the day. They wake up in the night……. Is it hibernation? …no Nocturnal!" When asked if he knew any other nocturnal animals he answered, "Owls, spiders, hedgehogs ………(Zak paused and thought)…… and what about crabs? Are they nocturnal?"

Eloise

"This is my special photo, it is me and Lauren when we were little, we have been friends for such a long time."

"We used to go dancing but then we got too big."

"I'm going to Lapland for Christmas, it will be nice when we open presents on holiday."

"First we will see Santa and then we will see the Elves."

"This is my special comfort teddy. I had him when he was a baby – he's not shiny anymore. I still keep him – he's special to me."

Jack

Children looking through books at the creative table.

"I am going to do an aeroplane because it can fly over the cold countries and I will be able to look down to see the bears and see what they are doing. I want to write planes."

Teacher sounds it out. He wrote label plans. He went on to talk about helicopters. Wrote hecopts.

Molly made an egg from paper.

"I've made a bed for my egg. She fell out of bed and bumped her head so I've put a plaster on!"

"Eggs need to be safe you know?"

Daisy used the mobile phone in the jungle campsite. She said number names as she pressed the buttons.

"Hello, it's Daisy. Yes, I'm in the jungle, are you coming to visit?" Yes, yes, it's really hot here and we've got a baby tiger... ok, bye!"

Molly got her file out from the shelf.
She laid it open on the floor.

"I remember doing this" she commented on a photo.

"Oh, look, I'm not very good at writing here - ha, ha – I'm much better than that now."

Enjoys looking at own work and noting changes in ability with pride.

"I've just rescued this baby from a fire, that's what firemen do, and cats that get stuck in trees."

"You be the ambulance lady – so you can take the baby to hospital (passes baby to P)"

"Quick, there's another fire, I need to go – Nee Naw Nee Naw – I'm coming!"

The children were very excited when they saw the tadpole and frog habitat area. They looked with care and interest and talked about what they could see. The group had been working on life cycles and had looked at factual books.

Erica - "I can see 1,2,3,4,5,6,7,8,9,10!!! They've all turned big with this .... max-i-fyer glass! These are frogspawn eggs. They go into frogs. They're going to get legs next. Remember from that book yesterday."

Caden tried to count the tadpoles - "I guess 60. One's swimming. Look how fast he is! He's wiggling his tail. Look, the magni-glass makes it bigger. It's come out of a cocoon.....no, an egg."

Erica - "Is that the frog egg? Because it's see through and has black beans inside."

Caden - "I think it is.......... Tadpoles come out of that jelly and then tadpoles turn into frogs. We eat jelly but not that one, yuck! We ate jelly at my birthday last week."

The 2 children moved on to work in the frog habitat.

Erica found a small plastic frog - "Mine's got red eyes. He must be allergic! Remember about the colours in that big book."

Caden - very seriously - "Is it poisonous? Red means it's got poison in it."

Madison enjoys working alongside others. She particularly enjoys working with adults.
She mirrors what they do, asks questions and answers relevant questions appropriately.
Whilst working in the garden with Gardening Grandad...

Are these ones weeds? Shall I pull them up...? How do you know what are the weeds? (GG You learn which ones when you have been gardening a long time like me?)
"Oh will I know when I am a big girl? It's o.k you can show me before im big."

We are building a house Mrs G. This is where the door is (pointed to an opening) We need to put the roof on. Balance it here, L you need to hold that bit, yep that is it.
It is getting higher and higher.
There! It is ready come on let's go inside. We need a blanket to sit on so it is comfy.

Snapshot obs of children outside building a den independently. Confidently communicating with teacher.

Ben -
We had a film
yesterday about a creature.
Guess what it was I'll give
you a clue, it is simila
to a spider. Has legs, can
you guess? Do you need
another clue?

Snapshot observation of
informed conversation.
Ben is using correct tense, able
to engage the listener by using
his questions. He is beginning
to connect ideas by saying it is
similar to a spider.

Joel has just read to his
class teacher and is told
to go and get a sticker
for good reading.

He passes the TA and
explains "I've got three
stickers and if anyone
thinks I am stealing it,
I'm not, because they
can ask Harry because
I have just read to get
my sticker."

Qobid was measuring things with a metre stick. He measured the trays He said "the trays are bigger than the stick. It's 90 metres. I mean 90 centimetres". Qobid measured a basket "I think this is 5 cm" He measured himself. "I am bigger" he said. "but not as big as the school" He held the metre stick in the air to see if he could reach the ceiling. "I'm not big enough" Miss Chamberlain asked Qobid who was the biggest out of her, Miss Williamson and Qobid. Qobid thought Miss Chamberlain was the biggest He stood back to back with Ethan. "Ethan is bigger than me this much", he said, using his hands to show how much.

EYFS Profile exemplification for the level of learning and development expected at the end of the EYFS

Physical development

ELG04 – Moving and handling

> **Children show good control and co-ordination in large and small movements. They move confidently in a range of ways, safely negotiating space. They handle equipment and tools effectively, including pencils for writing.**

Charlie waited his turn!

Charlie moved with confidence along the logs before jumping safely into a space. He told his friend to 'wait, so you don't crash.'

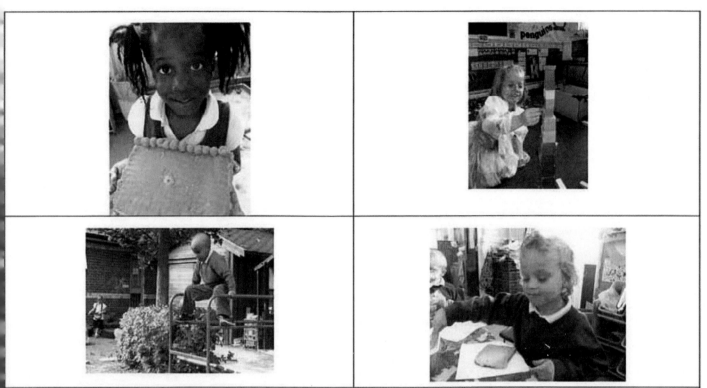

Ashley spent a very long time at the play dough table. She flattened a large portion of playdough out on to a small tray. She then used her finger to carefully make indentations across the dough in a regular pattern. She then found some more dough and rolled it in to small balls by placing small quantities on the palm of her hand and using circular movements made lots of small ball shapes. She carefully placed them next to each other ensuring that they touched in order to leave no space between them. She put a candle holder in the middle and declared that she had made a birthday cake.

Honey was able to balance small bricks on top of each other to make a very tall construction. She told the adult that you have to be very careful that you put one on top of the other and that it was best to try and cover the whole of the underneath brick so that it would balance and stay in place.

Heiden was able to demonstrate good control and co-ordination by placing his feet on the bar of the apparatus and hold a balance for some considerable time. He was then able to jump off from the equipment and land safely, bending his knees on to a mat.

Jamie used a plastic knife with great accuracy by placing it at the edge of the butter tub and pushing a small amount of butter on to the knife. He was then able to spread the butter on to the bread by turning his wrist and using the flat side of the knife he moved it over the whole slice of bread ensuring that it went into the corners.

Physical development

During den building, working as a group, children have the opportunity to practise tying knots, manipulating string and allowing them to apply their controlled and coordinated skills.

Samuel: Jumping from the plank into the large sauce, judging where to land so it doesn't tip over make him fall down. He practices this and then shows his friend how to do this safely. He extends this so he can jump from the saucer and jump across to the shelter pole using the rocking motion. He arranges the apparatus until he is happy

Oscar encouraged his two friends to join him in his 'super hero den', "We need to make messages for Intelliwrite (the class fictional character who leaves them challenges eachday) he will read them when we go home. He will like pictures. Get scissors, Ethan help us." Oscar carefully cut shapes he had drawn on card, following the lines he had drawn. He then pinned them carefully to the display board under the table.
Oscar likes his art work to be displayed in the class "So my friends can see my pictures."

A. confidently used the giant spinning top to roll his body in a large circular movement.

Jaden rode the two-wheeled bike around the outside classroom (child initiated). It took a lot of effort to get started, but once going he was able to ride the bike in straight lines and could keep his balance around shallow bends. When he reached the fence he got off the bike and turned it around by hand.

Jaden rode the two wheeled bike quickly around the outside classroom, showing good control despite his speed (child initiated).

Jaden kicked a football around the outside classroom and also kicked the football to Louis, showing that he could control the direction and speed of the ball (child initiated).

Jaden enjoyed bouncing a ball. He was able to control the ball well and could move his hand and/ or body nearer to the ball when necessary. Jaden could also adjust the force of his 'pats' to keep the ball bouncing. When I asked him how he had learnt to bounce a ball, he told me that his brother had taught him (child initiated).

Jaden was able to move forwards and backwards on the stepper, although he was a bit wobbly! Child initiated

Jaden and Louis asked me to come to see what they had been practising. They showed me how they could now do rolls around the bar on the climbing frame (child initiated).

Harriet performed somersaults over the bar on the climbing frame (child initiated).

Jaden enjoyed his time in the adventure playground at Longleat and confidently climbed the net

Jaden was keen to try the 'Loopy' and succeeded in coordinating his arms to make it move (child initiated).

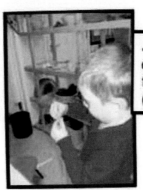

Jaden threaded pasta onto a piece of string to make a necklace (adult led activity).

Jaden filled a peg board with pegs, easily holding and placing the pegs into the holes (child initiated).

Harriet kept her balance on the balance walkway. Child initiated

Jaden chose to use the Numicon shapes and fitted them together on a board.

Jaden chose to paint a picture and controlled the paintbrush well, carefully painting around each colour.

Harriet copied the numerals from 1 – 10 onto a whiteboard (child initiated).

Harriet cut out a circle, drew a face on it and told me that it was her Mummy (child initiated).

Harriet enjoyed stepping from one log to another. I challenged her to jump between the logs and she then jumped from one log to another, just stepping between two logs on the way. Child initiated

Observation:
Yash-Raj is outside building with the hollow blocks. He picks up a large block and places it at a right angle to another large block. He collects smaller blocks and arranges them in a straight line. He uses two wooden planks to make a ramp to the structure which is now L-shaped. Yash-Raj goes to and from the trolley where the blocks are kept, collecting them one at a time and laying them in the structure. He collects a square piece which will not fit in the space left; he puts it on its side.

Observation:
Yash-Raj is playing "beans" in the hall with a group of children. When the teacher shouts "runner bean" the children all run in the space. Yash-Raj doges around the other children whilst running and when signalled he stops very quickly. He makes sure that he does not bump into anyone." During the session, Yash-Raj changes direction whilst running, hops, skips and jumps. He continues to run and move at the same rate throughout the 10 minute session.

Observation:
Yash-Raj is outside, running in and out of the cones which have been placed at intervals. Another boy is running through the cones in the opposite direction and Yash-Rah swerves to avoid him. He runs up the 3-step staircase and leaps off the top, landing on the mat on both feet.

Millie was able to balance and travel across the trim trail without wobbling or falling off. She then was able to travel across the stilts to complete the task. She knew that she needed to put her feet on the correct stilt and then which foot to move at a time. She knew that to help her hold her balance she should hold on to the upright posts.

When using the computer independently Heiden was able to use the mouse to scroll across the screen accurately and click on the icon to open up the application.

Ellie was able to grip a fine paint brush between her thumb and fingers and then dip the brush into her palette and make desired paint marks on the paper.

Outside Tristan was playing with his friends, they had got the builders equipment out of the shed. He said to one of the other children *"We need to get some sand to build a wall."*

He pushed the wheelbarrow over to the sandpit whilst carefully holding onto his spade. When he got to the sandpit, he and two friends filled the wheelbarrow with sand and pushed it back to where they were building the wall.

They then tried to use the dry sand to go between the bricks, watching on as the sand ran off the bricks. Then Tristan said *"I know, we need water"* and wheeled the sand over to the water butt and used the tap to fill the wheelbarrow up with water to make a wet mix.

He then pushed this back to the 'wall' without spilling the mixture. He said to his friends *"Now it is cement!"*

He began to shovel the mixture onto the bricks he had laid in a line. As his friends joined back in he said *"Okay Ethan, put your brick on top of this one."* (Pointed to a position on top of where he had laid bricks.) He watched to make sure Ethan put the brick where he wanted it, before saying *"Come on, it's not tall enough yet."*

They continued to build the wall until they had used up all of the bricks. Tristan said *"Now we need to clean up, let's be the clean-up team!"* So they washed off the bricks with water and brooms.

T carefully rolls out the play dough before coiling it up to form fossils. He selects a number of different tools (from the continuous provision), explores and experiments with them in the play dough and eventually adds the marks with his preferred tools.

"Look! I can screw the nuts onto the bolts just like Grandad!"

lunchtime supervisor's voice!

Thomas proudly shows me (lunchtime supervisor) that he had written his name in the mud.

A's dad brought in a selection of nuts, bolts, washers and screws, (inspired by a robot story that A had borrowed from the library).

A and A-L confidently handled them, picking out individual nuts and washers and carefully sorting them into different categories.

Displaying high levels of involvement, B carefully used fine tweezers to sort the beans.

"I can make a kite, I know, I will attach my flyer to my coat and run with it." Alice

"I know, the air can go through there and it can fly!"

Ishak independently put on his hat, gloves, waterproofs and wellies to play in the snow.
He enjoyed using the 'vegetable box' to slide down the hills. He repeatedly explored this activity looking for the 'best' hill. Ishak shared the sledge with Jessica and waited patiently for his next turn.
"I like this slide the best cos it's really fast. You go zoom!
The fastest ones are the tallest hills."

Keira has been determind to master the new balance board today! She has been on it for over twenty minutes! She finally realised she could use her arms to steady herself for long enough for me to get the camera and take a picture!

Observation:
Yash-Raj is outside. He drags a plastic rocker over to near the climbing frame and very carefully balances on it to launch himself onto the frame. He swings on the bar and onto a chair which had previously been placed there for the "driver". He walks across the rope netting, hardly looking down to see where his feet are. He swings round the pole with a delighted smile on his face and lands with both feet on the platform below. Yash-Raj uses the equipment to challenge himself and take risks, but is careful at all times and does not try to do anything which is beyond his ability.

Observation:
Yash-Raj is outside building with the hollow blocks. He picks up a large block and places it at a right angle to another large block. He collects smaller blocks and arranges them in a straight line. He uses two wooden planks to make a ramp to the structure which is now L-shaped. Yash-Raj goes to and from the trolley where the blocks are kept, collecting them one at a time and laying them in the structure. He collects a square piece which will not fit in the space left; he puts it on its side.

Observation:
Earlier in the month, Ruby enjoyed playing with the small wooden hammer and pins set, tapping shapes into position. She is then confident to choose to use the bigger tools at the woodwork table. She carefully chooses a small nail, a block of wood, and the large hammer. She screws her face up in concentration and hammers the nail carefully into the block, making sure that she keeps her fingers away from the hammer. "I did that very carefully," she says. "I didn't want to hurt my fingers."

EYFS Profile exemplification for the level of learning and development expected at the end of the EYFS

Physical development

ELG05 – Health and self-care

Children know the importance for good health of physical exercise, and a healthy diet, and talk about ways to keep healthy and safe. They manage their own basic hygiene and personal needs successfully, including dressing and going to the toilet independently.

Corben read out the instructions to make a sandwich - from the jam.

When asked why we don't lick our fingers Corben replied:

"There's germs in your mouth and you don't want to get them on your sandwich."

During a visit from a refuse lorry, A asks the refuse collector how he keeps his hands clean when he is handling people's rubbish, demonstrating that he has a clear understanding of why good hygiene is important. A shows the ability to transfer his knowledge and apply it to a new context. A is interested as the refuse collector shows him how the small sink works.

B said:

"I'm going to put my milk carton in the plastic recycle tub."

Daniel was sitting at the snack table eating bananas and declared that they were his favourite fruit. He told the group that his mummy had told him that they were full of vitamins and were very healthy and good for you.

After playing in the outdoor clasroom Daniel declared that he was hot and sweaty. 'All that running about has made me thirsty'. He then independently took himself off to the rolling snack table where he poured himself a drink of water. 'That's better, now I'm not thirsty anymore, he said to the adult.

On a cold day Ellie went to the cloakroom to put on her outdoor clothes. She returned to the classroom having managed to put on her coat, hat, gloves and scarf. She asked an adult to help her with some buttons as 'It is cold today and I need to have my coat done up to stop me being cold'.

On the given signal to get ready for snack time Tyler took himself to the cloakroom. He pressed the soap dispenser button and put a small amount of soap on his hand. He rubbed his hands together and then pressed the tap and rinsed his hands with water. He then used the drier to dry his hands. On finishing he knew he was ready for snack time.

Little Star Voucher

On .... (date) ..... Mia .... (child's name)

Achieved.. Got out of the bath, dried

Put her P.J's on and .... ☺ .... at home.
brushed her hair all by
herself

We are all very proud and said 'you are a little star'!

Halle
"Vitamin C is
in carrots ....fruit
makes you grow....
I love spag. bolog.
I have it in the
restaurant"

Ⓙ
"I use mouthwash
when everyone else
can't and I use
mouthwash before I
come to school. You
have to do this (action).
You put a bit in + spit it
out
Its good for your mouth +
teeth"

"I need to
wash my hands
now" Eloise said
after touching the
hamster.

Halle
While discussing
eating fruit Halle
said "It's just like
drinking orange juice
but you have to brush
your teeth because
of sugar"

"My dad says mum
needs to give me
more healthy and
strong food to get
healthy and strong like
fruit and not junk
food." (His teresas didn't fix)

Alfred sat at the snack table and told the adult that he loved milk as it was good for you. He knew that it made his bones grow strong and healthy.

Joe was able to undress himself independently for PE. He was able to take his sweatshirt off by taking out one arm and then using his free arm to pull out the other arm.

Charlotte knew that when she was exploring in the wooded area outside that she was allowed to climb up on the bottom part of the trees but that it would not be safe for her to climb any higher as she may fall out of the tree if she went too high and that 'I might hurt myself and then I would need to go to the medical room'.

Samuel is too hot so he takes off his jumper:

"I'm going to hang my jumper on my peg."

Samuel gets his gloves and coat and dresses himself to go outside.

Kamran is able to put his coat on and do up the zip independently. He is also able to take his shoes off, put them on the shelf and put his wellies on by himself when going to play outside. (J.B.)

When playing with the large wooden blocks outside today, Harriet knew that the children needed to play carefully because; "if we fall down we might break our bones". S.R.

Whilst playing in the outdoor classroom, Julia said; "Mrs Carlier, I am hot. Can I take my coat off please?" L.C.

When looking at vegetables, Edward thought that we eat vegetables because; "they are delicious and they are healthy for you". L.C.

S.W. Esme was asked "can you tell me how to stay healthy?" Esme replied "you got to eat healthy food like apples and oranges and a drink of water. Do exercise. Then you keep healthy. You need sleep to get energy."

Kamran played with the large wooden blocks outside. Before he jumped from the structure the children had made he asked Thomas to move, keeping Thomas safe. S.R.

Whilst working on the wood work bench Nicholas independently took the safety goggles and put them on before he began to saw.

Observation:
Whilst in the home corner Nicholas independently changed into the Bob the Builder clothes. He was able to take off his own trousers and polo shirt and then put on Bobs shirt and dungarees. He then went over to the workbench and pretended to hammer some nails.

Alex is starting to recognise the changes that happen to his body when he is active.
He told me his heart gets faster and you get muscles

When planting the coriander seeds Nicholas said "At home I planted carrot and broccoli seeds with my brother. Mum said they are healthy and will be one of our five a day."

At the weekend we took Nicholas to Be Q to buy a hammer and a saw as he'd shown a real interest in woodwork at school. At the checkout, Nicholas said "Daddy I need some goggles to keep my eyes safe." So Nicholas and Dad went back to find some goggles.

Observation
After going to the toilet Harry can independently wash his own hands following the instructions on the wall. He also regularly reminds other class members.

"Mrs Bowers look the peas have grown. Pea pod. pea pod. pea pod" Nicholas laughs to himself. "Mrs Bowers peas are good for you aren't they... they are one of your 5 a day"

Qobid formed some brilliant shapes today. Here he is showing off his fantastic balancing skills!

Qobid was able to climb and balance with great skill and imagination!

Qobid told me his tummy makes a funny loud noise when he's hungry.
We talked about eating to be big and strong.
"I'm big and strong because I sleep good and eat well and do some excercises" said Qobid. I asked him what excercises he does.
Qobid showed me his star jumps, push ups, and body twists.

Qobid helped to cut the fruit for the snack table. He used the knife carefully and was able to cut the apple into regular sized pieces.

Qobid manages his own personal needs. He uses the toilet independently & flush and washes his hands afterwards. Qobid knows to wash his hands before eating

Qobid made soup today in the water tray! He used lots of different utensils and pots and pans.
"It takes a long time to make it, then it will be hot". Qobid told me that his soup had vegetables in 'because they are good for you'.

Qobid chose to play outside today. He put on his coat and fastened it himself He chose some wellies and put them on, then put his shoes on the welly stand out of the way.

Qobid sat at the snack table with his friends, talking about which foods are healthy.
"fruit is good for your tummy, but I cant bite pears because my teeth are too soggy".
Qobid told me that sweets and chocolate are not good because they make your teeth go bad'.

Qobid chose to ride on the large bike outdoors today. He was able to steer and control the bike and slowed down when someone crossed his path

"I can get my coat on myself but it's a bit hard when the sleeve's inside out."

"I go to gymnastics, I can do press ups and cartwheels, exercise makes me healthy and strong."

"Handstands are good exercise, and stretching. I do warm ups to keep me fit and so I don't hurt my muscles."

Leni goes to the toilet independently, washes and dries her hands and puts on her coat, she fastens the zip and goes outside.
"It's frosty out there, I'd better be careful so I don't slip."

Milk is good for you, it makes your bones strong.

Fruit is good for you but I don't like it, I have vitamins to keep me healthy cos I don't like veg either!"

"You have to do exercise otherwise you won't get strong."

Observation:
Ruby is part of a group of children sitting around the table having snacks and talking together. Ruby pours water from the jug into the cups. "You need to walk to school twice a day," she says pointing to the signs about Walk on Wednesday (WOW). "You need to drink water every day and exercise every day to keep fit. I like vegetables – you need to eat vegetables as well." Yaqub looks at her and says "sweets and crisps are not good for you." "Only a little," says Amadon. Ruby finishes her apple and cup of water. She takes her cup over to the sink – turns the tap on and washes her cup. She places her cup on the draining board and picks up all the cups which have been left in the sink. She places them all on the draining board. Then she washes her hands with soap and pulls the paper towels from the holder on the wall. She dries her hands and throws the paper towels into the bin.

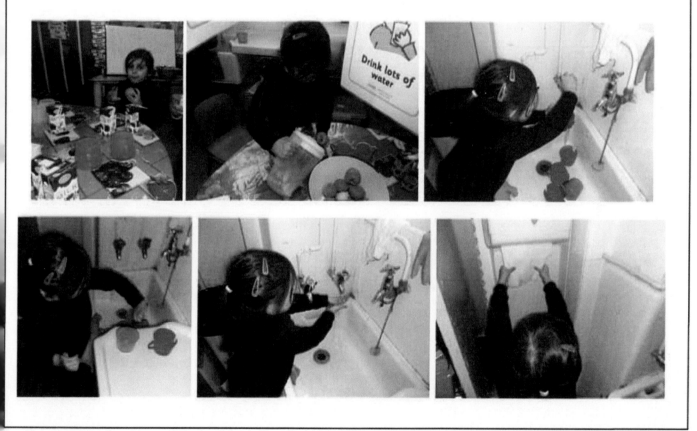

EYFS team meeting:
Ruby's teacher checks with the rest of the team that Ruby is managing the toilet independently and that she is able to put on and take off her coat. Ruby has also been observed helping another child with the buttons on her cardigan.

EYFS Profile exemplification for the level of learning and development expected at the end of the EYFS

Personal, social and emotional development

ELG06 – Self-confidence and self-awareness

Children are confident to try new activities, and say why they like some activities more than others. They are confident to speak in a familiar group, will talk about their ideas, and will choose the resources they need for their chosen activities. They say when they do or don't need help.

- Context - In the work shop area the children have to think of a way that super heroes, who have lost their powers, can rescue people from a burning building.

1 'I've made a springer so they can jump up. I've used a tube. I used sellotape to make the string stick.'

2 A jet – 'I got a black box and I stuck this on and left it because it had to dry to stay on there. I put those two things on there. I used sticky tape for this bit so the glue is not strong enough and it will fall off. They are the wings and they make it stay in the air.'

3 'I'm going to make a flying ship for spider man because he has lost his powers. I am going to use a box and a yoghurt pot.'

4   I'm going to make a trampoline so superman can fly, with a tissue box and paper. I'm going to use sellotape so it will make it strong and it won't take a long time to dry. I put paper in there to make it bouncier.

5 'Rocket – It could fly straight up to the building. I used an elastic band so I could keep the paper on. '

6 'I made a ladder for superman. These are the handles on this side. J used sellotape because glue didn't work.'

As part of a group, Ben thoughtfully collected together the resources he needed to create a rock pool for the dinosaurs discussing with his friends which rocks would be the best size and why, sharing his ideas on how to stop the water running away, and asking for help when he needed to move the largest of the stones into position.

Context
After writing letters to their family the class walked to the local post office to buy stamps and post their letters.

Observation
Alex was confident to ask the lady at the counter for his stamp saying "Please can I have a second class stamp?" When told it would be 36p he handed over the four ten pence coins he had previously been given. He collected his change and the stamp and said "Thank you"

HA decided to try different ways of moving around the obstacle course. Initially his friends helped him get on and off the tyres, but then he realised he could do it by himself. Well done!

Jumps repeatedly into the puddle he holds hands with AM before jumping They add a tyre and jump into the tyre from the wall

Was playing a game with some friends. They were pretending to be chased by invisible baddies. He climbed up the tree to escape them. "You can't get me," he said, then jumped down and ran off saying "I'm ok, I can do it."

Shared Parental Observations of learning outside of school

Child's name: Iz

Name of person writing observation:

Relationship of person to child: Father

Date of observation:

Observation Notes:
Iz attended a football training session for Netherton Football Club held at "The Grange", Peterborough.
He interacted with the other boys playing, and with the coach.
Iz : dribbled the ball, then took a penalty shot. The coach shouted "well done", to Iz".
Iz looked very proud, and pleased with what he had achieved.
Iz was learning how to be part of a team, and pass the ball to the others in his team.
At the end of the session he was happy and decided that he felt his skills were improving.

JA got himself ready to go into the digging area. He put on a protective jacket and trousers and wellington boots. He used different tools to loosen and then collect mud.   "I'm making some yummy food for the worms. I love digging in the dirt and doing messy stuff 'cause I don't get dirty wearing my suit". He pretended to add different ingredients, mixing it all together.

VE independently initiated this activity selecting and arranging different pieces of paper to make diva lamps. Had dressed in Indian dress and talked to class about Diwali and what he had done at home to celebrate.

Context and content of observation:
OUTSIDE AREA

C1 + C2 have a hoola hoop and are experimenting with different ways of moving them. MA approaches and after watching his friends, decides to join in. He tries standing the hoop upright, then spinning it. They roll them to see whose hoop travels the furthest.
MA notices a fixed pole: Let's try to get them on that!
He aims his hoop and successfully throws it over the pole. His friends cheer and then try it.
I ask them how they could make it even more difficult.
MA: I know let's stand back more.
He takes 2 steps back and throws the hoop but misses the pole.
MA: I'll have to throw it higher next time.
They continue playing hoopla.
MA decides to score how many times he can throw it on the pole.
MA: I've got 6 points now!

got resources (costume, bag, envelopes. etc) ready + acted as a postman following our trip yday to the post office. Went round the area delivering letters to his friends staying in role.

KE
made a book. She tried to staple the pages together but the stapler had run out of staples. She used a hole punch to make 2 holes and threaded ribbon through. She asked me to tie a knot.

DI
was able to show other children how to make a foil boat. He gave clear instructions. "First fold the ends up so they stand up. Make the shape of a boat. Good! Now put it in the water to see if it sinks or floats!"

HA selects materials he wants from collage box. Returns items when he's finished with it.

JG
Look how many chairs I've got out counted them 1-11. I'm good at counting but sometimes I get it wrong.

CH was very excited when we introduced the pulley. He loves playing in the water - usually goes in every day. He attached the full bucket to the pulley and said "this is great, I wonder what would happen if I let go of the rope?"

Star of the week

Alex was star of the week and decided to talk to the class about football. Alex told the class how he is a keen footballer and goes to the out of school football club in the village and having a season ticket for Sheffield Wednesday. He brought in his football kit and talked through what each item was. He also told us about how his great grandad was a professional footballer.

"I love going to football with my dad. Mummy and Georgia don't come with us because they don't like football!"

Antonia confidently attempted to hoola hoop & persisted even when she found it difficult. She practised every day and was thrilled when she could eventually do it.

Alex asked a friend to show him how to make the 'twinkle stars'

Alex was asked to fill the bowl with water. He asked his friend to help him as he couldn't turn the tap & hold the bowl at the same time

These monkeys are much smaller than the ones in the other cage. They look very soft and furry!

OK worked with his friend to clean the guinea pig's cage. He pretended to be a zoo keeper + shook the food. "Come on! Feeding time!" He later waited for his turn to handle the guinea pig which he did gently.

Starting point... A trip to the zoo.

"This is lots of fun! I like playing with this. I can go really, really fast when I press this (the bar)." This was at the zoo play area he had never ridden one before

OK enjoyed choosing and mixing different ingredients. He related it back to the zoo. "Let's pretend we're making food for all the animals. I'm making this one for the monkeys 'cause they like sticky food!"

Olaf's Story....

The next day after the zoo trip, OF went on the computer, logged in and inserted these animal pictures into a Word document. He said that he liked the animals on the top line but not the ones on the bottom line. I asked about the camel and he nodded and said 'top'.
Ae.

As part of a class activity focussing on things the children had enjoyed during the year, OF chose a speech bubble voice recorder. He spoke into it and then chose to write what he had said. "You can hear it and see it now." he said and gave it to the teacher.

OF had never been to the zoo before but was very excited as he loves animals.

OF talked about the goat's soft coat. He said he had stroked a goat when he visited Sacrewell farm with his dad. He had fed the lambs and said it was 'lots of fun'.

OF picked up his clipboard after he had finished his picnic lunch. He drew some of the animals he had seen and asked MF for some help to write the word 'animals'. When he had finished he told MF the picture was for his mummy because she had been feeling poorly and a bit sad.

Drew this picture a month later and said to a friend "Do you remember ages ago when we went to the zoo? We went on the bus and saw loads of animals.

I like drawing animals

"It's a garden". Z worked with M to build 'a garden' using lego bricks and connectors. Shared ideas and resources.

Child Z

"We are making a castle wall...We need to share the bricks." Said Z as the boys started to take the girls' bricks.

"We've got a burglar alarm in our castle" and she pointed to a yellow brick.

Working closely with M, Z put out all the domes to create a play area outside. They took turns to place the domes around the edge.

Worked with Q to make a bed for the 3 bears' house using own ideas and materials self selected from the creative area.

"You put the pillow here. We need to stick it down." Then Z made a bow to make the bow to make the bed 'look like mummy bear's bed'.

During child initiated activity, Z directed the play to make the three bear's house using large plastic bricks. They made an outline with plastic bricks, then used recycled materials to add 'cobbles'. They left a gap for the 'doorway'. As Z was adding drainpipes, she said " Can you help me! It's too heavy to carry on my own."

K led a game of Simon says outdoors with a small group of friends. She explained the rules and reminded children to follow them during the game.

Selected a paint programme to use, but it was slow to start.

"It's loading"   Z

"Everyone in the street was cheering" Z

[The Royal Wedding]

Manisha, Poppy and Ellie worked
in a group to make an angel for the
Christmas display in the hall.
They discussed which materials to
use for each part of the picture.
Manisha suggested using handprints
for the hair.

Home/school diary entries

On Saturday we went to Sundown. It was really good fun. The barrel
ride was the best.   Daddy got squirted by the crocodile and Uncle
Glen lost his sunglasses in the water.

On Monday night it was Manisha's Brownie promise evening. She
said her promise to the rest of the group and got given badge sash
and a group badge. She did really well, we were very proud of her!

Context
Child initiated outdoor play

Observation
Manisha is in the outdoor area with the den making
box. She shouts "Poppy, help me, I'm building a
den to hide in." Poppy runs over to join her. "Put
this blanket over the this box." Manisha unfolds
the blanket and Poppy helps her drape it over the
box. Manisha - "How can we fix it to the fence?"
Poppy looks into the box and gets out the peg box.
She takes one corner if the blanket and pegs it to
the metal fence. Together they peg one edge of
the blanket across the fence. Manisha crawls under blanket and sits on the floor in the den.

EYFS Profile exemplification for the level of learning and development expected at the end of the EYFS

Personal, social and emotional development

ELG07 – Managing feelings and behaviour

Children talk about how they and others show feelings, talk about their own and others' behaviour, and its consequences, and know that some behaviour is unacceptable. They work as part of a group or class, and understand and follow the rules. They adjust their behaviour to different situations, and take changes of routine in their stride.

Fobhan went around the class as a policeman giving people high fives if they were making good decisions.

The children worked together to group the different types of fruit – blackcurrants, cherries, raspberries and blackberries. They supported each other, for example, BW said, "I don't know what his is" and MF answered "It's a blackcurrant, they go in that bowl." BW smiled to show his appreciation for the help given by MF. The children then took it in turns to tip the contents of the bowls into the blender and add yogurt to make fruit smoothies to sell to the Year 1 pupils later on that day.

'This painting is about faces showing you what they mean,' said Alice. She went on to explain to Ms Hill 'that the green face was showing it was happy, the red one was sad, the purple one wasn't really happy or sad and the blue one was really mad!!!' 'I got the idea from the red and green faces we use to show our friends how we feel.'

Alice and Ellen worked together with the Bee-bots. They were able to switch them on and off, knew that they were powered by batteries and that they were controlling the Beebots by pressing the buttons. They could make it go forward and backwards and clear the previous instructions too. 'We are taking it in turns to go,' said Alice 'I'm good at taking turns and sharing!'

- 'We can't go outside on the climbing frame today because it's slippy. We need to make a sign to tell everyone to be careful! The Frog bin tells us not to go on there.'

- 'We don't play fight in the playground because someone may get hurt.'

- 'I like to dance' said ----. I like different music though this sounds funny. Mrs C asks ---- how dancing makes her feel. "Dancing makes me feel happy because I can do it with friends!"

- ---- and a friend have invented a game. The friend is spinning in the middle and he runs round. 'Stop' she calls and he does. Repeats this several times then the friend says 'your turn'. They swap places. ---- spins and calls stop then names the 2d shapes she has stopped on, 'circle, square, '

- --- worked with a group of friends negotiating how to transfer water from the low tray to the other. They are shared ideas and tried lifting, turning, holding pipes and pouring.

- Child was dancing to the music. She was waving ribbons to move to the music 'dancing makes me happy'.

> Edward was fishing for letters in the water tray when Corey wanted to join in. Corey said; "Hey! You've got them all!" and Edward immediately said; "You can share mine" and gave some to Corey.

> When creating the class rules the children said:
>
> Lottie "help each other."
>
> Lance "we must walk."
>
> Esme "look after each other and look after the books."
>
> Leia "share the toys."
>
> Jake "be quiet, sit still and be kind."
>
> Ellie "to be the speaker first and then listen."

> Will said "it's not nice to hit cause it hurts."

When playing on the climbing frame Ben said to Dylan "be careful at the top cause it can be dangerous."

Gracie washed her paint palette up without being asked. Harriet also helped to tidy up by bringing the dirty water pots to the sink to be replaced with fresh water.

- Conversation with Mrs Drew at the beginning of the day regarding how Libby is adjusting to having a new baby in the family.

"Libby is coping really well. She found it a bit difficult in the first week or so, but during the holiday she has been really helpful and has enjoyed playing with Tilly. She was fine about coming back to school. Tilly is at home with her daddy this morning and Libby gave her a big hug and kiss when she left. I'm really proud of how she has adjusted."

Sonny was playing with the dinosaurs. He came up to Mrs W and said "Callum has got the big dinosaur and I want it" Mrs W - "You've got lots of little dinosaurs though. If you have the big one as well Callum won't have any. How will that make him feel?" Sonny - "He will be sad." Mrs W - "What do you think you could do to make you both feel better?" Sonny - "I could ask him to swap some small dinosaurs for the big one." Mrs W - "That sounds like a good idea."

Sonny asks and Callum is happy to swap.

Jack and Libby are playing with the zebra crossing and the lollipop stick in the outdoor area. Libby has put on the lollipop persons coat. Jack attempts to cross the crossing before Libby has stopped Henry on one of the bikes. She shouts, "No, Jack you must not cross before I stop the traffic. You will get run over!"

Filling water tray using the hose pipe he say's to a c in the group "Quick turn the tap off else is will be too full and spill everywhere".

after getting unchanged, he made sure his suit was turned the right way round "Look Miss! It's all ready for tomorrow now!"

WOW!

Write something that your child has done well this weekend. Bring it in and put it on our WOW board! ☺

JA   has been a star all   weekend because he has   helped tidy up when he   was asked to.

RI jumped in the muddy hole. He laughed as he landed and had a good splash in the mud. He got out and went to the back of the line to wait for another turn.

Context and content of observation:
PLAYING FOOTBALL

A child comes to me crying saying that IZ has kicked him.
IZ: Sorry!
He comes over to me.
IZ: We are playing football and I went for the ball but kicked his foot by accident. I said sorry.
IZ looked upset that he had hurt his friend. He put his arm around his shoulders and led him back to the game of football.

Drew picture as part of
risk assessment for trip to the
zoo. 'Stay with an adult and hold hands'
'Put seatbelts on'. 'Don't shout! You will scare
the animals'.

L said 'My Dad
will be really
proud of me now I
can write my own
name.'

Walking back from
church L noticed that
Noah was not holding
adults hand as
she was helping children
to cross the road. L
who was already with
a partner held childs
hand until the adult
had returned.

I think Alex feels
sad because he
just sniffed like
this... (he then
demonstrated)

Whilst building a
model with two friends
the child broke the
model and said
sorry. L said Oh that's
ok because you
told me.

EYFS Profile exemplification for the level of learning and development expected at the end of the EYFS

Personal, social and emotional development

ELG08 – Making relationships

> Children play cooperatively, taking turns with others.
> They take account of one another's ideas about how to organise their activity. They show sensitivity to others' needs and feelings, and form positive relationships with adults and other children.

Snapshot Observation

Child John _____ Date _____

Thomas was crying.
JC "Miss Vaughan, shall I wipe
Thomas' tears away with my
scarf?"

Snack time: Polly helped give out the
snack and helped the nursery
children cut their toast. One child
was very upset and she distracted
her by singing a song.

Road Sweeping.
Daniel W.

"Like TV Burp!"

I was watching him and
Archie trying to get
around with a long brush
on the two-seater bike.

I said it was like
watching telly.

Snapshot Observation

Child Charlotte . _____ Date _____

OG- "Erm, its not fair, we've
got 19 blocks but
they've got more.

OG- "This is where the dogs come
in and when they get
bigger, you can take it off."
(Blocks)

> Context: The role play area had been developed into an Animal clinic linked to a recent visit by a vet. Child S chatted to the practitioner as she played.

What happens/happened:

S was dressed as a vet in the Animal Clinic, playing alone.
"Look I'm a vet!" she pointed to her uniform.
I handed her 3 tortoises.
"What's the matter with these?" she said.
I told her they were squashed under the cushion.
"Oh! That must mean it's serious!"
"I think they have broken hearts" she said as she examined them.
How are you going to fix that I asked.
"I'll put a plaster on and give them a big hug!"

- --- is throwing beanbags into a net with another girl. She is cheering the girl each time she gets one in the net.

- On the computer a child is offering advice as to where the number is and where it should go waiting his turn patiently.

- ---- and her friend made this car using the wooden blocks. 'We're going somewhere nice for lunch', she told the adult.

- 'Do you like my sunglasses' ----- showed how she made her glasses from stickle bricks.

- Helping another child get across the balancing beams on the playground. She's holding her hand when she gets all the way across.

- A child was giving a friend a helping hand and reassurance (when walking along small posts), 'Its ok you can do it, I'm not going to let go!'

This certificate is awarded to
Eva

For keeping the Golden Rule
We are kind and helpful

Eva noticed Francesca had painted a fantastic picture on the computer and went over to say 'That's a brilliant picture!'.
We have been talking a lot about how to be a good and kind friend.
Well done Eva!

E and B are exploring how the pulley system works. They have attached a bucket and have realised they can transport items from one side of the quad to the other.

E goes to the other side, "I'll put the things in."

B: "Okay – then I'll collect it on this side!"

They work well together, B saying "Okay, well done, good job" as it pulls from left to right.

M joins, "can I pull that?"

B: "Yes, okay, I'll sort the objects as they arrive."

B (to Miss Donald): "We are a good team."

E shouts that he wants to send some dinosaurs.

B is collecting items in milk crates. When the dinosaur arrives, it falls through.

M says they are "too small."

E says "oh..."

B says "just send the big ones."

E: "We haven't got many of them."

B: "That's okay, just keep going."

Using the big wooden blocks a group of children worked together to build a house.

Emily "Come on. Let's build a house."

Tom "This is a building site for building houses."

Charlie "Right Tom. I need a plank. It will help us."

Josh "Do you want one like this?"

Charlie "No. A long one."

Josh "Okay."

Emily picked up a long plank.

Emily "Where shall I put this?"

Josh "Here."

Charlie "Oh dear. It dropped on my foot. This (looking at the building) is not big enough yet."

John "Phew. This is heavy".

Emily "I'm putting the roof on now."

Charlie "Be careful".

Emily "We can crawl under."

Tom "We have to take the roof off to mend the water pipes. They have a leak."

John "Oh no. That means water will be coming out."

Josh "You have to be careful on the building site."

Tom "We are a good team."

Emily "This plank is too long."

Tom "Our house."

When Ella was 'stuck' on top of the large wooden block structure outside, Cameron told Ella how to get down. He described how she needed to turn around and how she should put her foot into one of the hollow blocks and then step down from there.

When Jaden and Julia were fishing for letters in the water tray they negotiated which fishing rods they had;
Julia to Jaden; "Do you want a red one? Can I have a blue one?"
Jaden gave Julia a blue fishing rod and Julia gave Jaden a red fishing rod.
Jaden said; "That's fair!" because they both had two fishing rods of the same colour.

When playing a number game, with a small group of children, Ben said "after me it is Poppy and then it's Olivia and then me again and then we go around again."

George came into school crying. Ben went up to George and said, "It is okay. I will look after you and play with you today. We will have fun".

Zak came up to me when we were playing outside and said; "There's something wrong with that girl (he pointed to Harriet). She's walking around like this" and showed me with his body that she was walking with her head down, her shoulders hunched and a sad face.

When Edward fell over outside, Kieron said; "are you O.K. Edward?"

HA loved pretending to be a dragon with his friend. They used a big tree branch as the tail. They took turns to be at the front.

KE showed concern when her friend fell off the tyres. She put her arm around her, took her to first aid + said "Are you ok? Does it hurt a lot?"

SH played with 3 friends setting the table in the outside house. They made sure there were 4 chairs, then SH handed out a cup, plate + cutlery to everyone. She looked around to make sure everyone had everything. Another friend came in the house and asked to play. SH said "Okay but you'll have to share my stuff." Later the friend finds a stool + SH tells her it's a good idea.

DI asked "Does he help with your shopping?" when a blind visitor came in with her dog.

HA worked out with his friends how to make an obstacle course. "Lets put the plank on top of that bit so it makes a slide" When his friend comes to help him lift it he says "Thanks LU! It's really heavy" Later HA shows his friends the different parts of the course. "Mias do you want a go? It's very tricky so be careful!"

Context: There is a deaf child in the class who wears hearing aids. Staff wear a microphone device to magnify sound for him. The class are learning some sign language.
RI: Mrs H, you wear the microphone so that DA can hear better.
Mrs H: That's right RI
RI: Why are you not wearing it today?
Mrs H: Because DA is at the Audiology clinic
RI: What's that?
Mrs H: It's where DA goes to get his ears and hearing aids checked.
RI: I hope he will be back this afternoon.

DI took it in turns to pull his friend in a wagon "Now you can sit down and I'll pull you!

Long observation during child-initiated activity

In the outdoor area Georgia and Lois are dancing on the stage. They each have ribbon sticks and move them to the rhythm of the music. When the track ends Lois says "Put that one on again, I like it." Georgia uses the rewind button and selects the track again. The girls both dance again. When the track finished Georgia says "Lets ask if we can make a video like Miss Tate did last week". Georgia goes inside and asks Miss Tate if we can use the video on her camera to record hers and Lois' dance. Miss Tate sets the camera to video mode and tells Georgia how to start recording. "Let's take it in turns. You video me first, then I'll do you." Georgia shows Lois how to start recoding. The girls record each others dance.

At the end of the day during story time, Georgia asked to show their video to the class.

At the snack table
Jemimah said
"I'm going to save this
apple for Kira because
she doesn't like oranges."

Observation:
During anti-bullying week Anya chose to make a friendship bracelet. "This is for Carrie, she's my best friend." She threaded the beads in a repeating pattern. When asked about her pattern she said "It's pink, purple, pink, purple. They are Carrie's favourite colours.

Cameron

"Will Mrs Johnson be back tomorrow? I've missed her today"

"I'm going to make her a get well card."

Hannah asked to put Georgia's name in The Golden Book because "She saw I was upset at playtime and asked me to play with her".

I was in the Golden Book

L could not remember how to write his name. He told his friend 'I can't remember the last bit'. His friend suggested he could find his name to copy.

During carpet time L said 'Shall I help Alex to make good choices I'm his friend now.' 'come on Alex' 'Good sitting now.'

"I did one, then J, then me. We take turns'. 'We should ask nicely 'cause we do that at school, don't we?'

I noticed that R was upset. The children were making lego aeroplanes. R gestured that she wanted an aeroplane. I said 'I will ask L if she doesn't want it anymore and give it to her or I will make her one.

Following a walk around the local village L worked with a friend to create their own village map. They worked together incorporating each other's ideas. "I'm doing a park and M's put a swimming pool there."

L noticed two boys who both wanted the spade. He suggested 'I know you could dig and then you.

EYFS Profile exemplification for the level of learning and development expected at the end of the EYFS

Literacy

ELG09 – Reading

Children read and understand simple sentences. They use phonic knowledge to decode regular words and read them aloud accurately. They also read some common irregular words. They demonstrate understanding when talking with others about what they have read.

Darcy reading in the outside classroom

Darcy was very pleased when she found a familiar book, "It's this one! It's about a mole. That's where it says mole." Then she added, "I can't read it yet because I don't know all the things yet." She turned to the first page and exclaimed with a broad smile, "Oh I can! That says baby. I've got a new baby! " She read most of the first 3 pages. She sound talked - it, it's, nest, big and help and used contextual clues for more complex words. She was supported with the word 'waited'. She then continued to tell me the story. She used picture clues, talked about the details in the illustrations and characters feelings. "I think that the little bird is his friend. That's good news. " She made connections and was very pleased with one page when she exclaimed, "He's reading a book like me!"
As she turned to the last page she said, "And that's the end."

Individual children take home Ben the Bear. Martha had taken home Ben. On her return to school she confidently read what her mum had written in the book that accompanies Ben home with the children.

'That word there says 'bear' said Milo. Milo was sharing a book with his sister Kitty.

"In books they use capitals, sometimes I copied them."

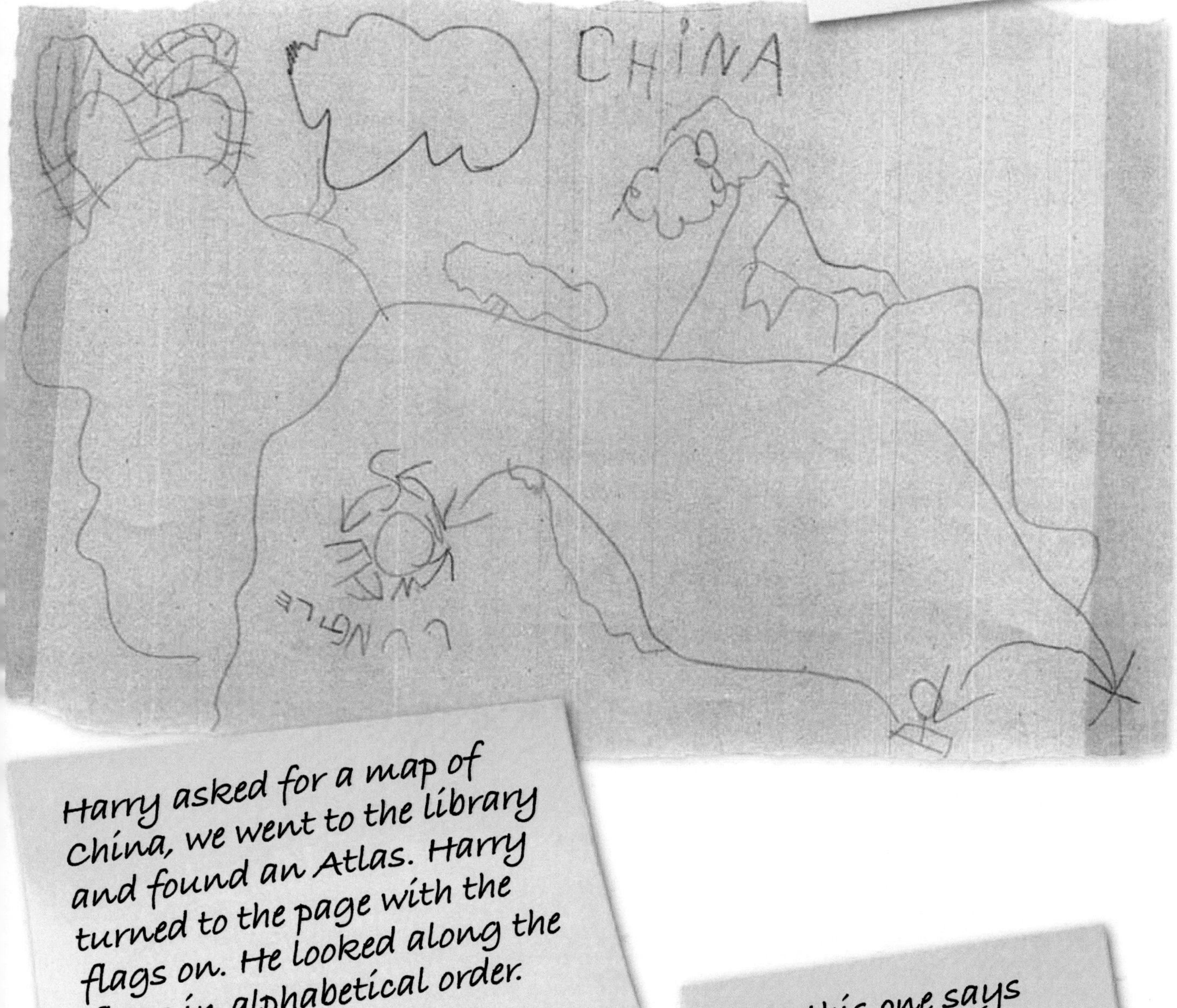

CHINA

JUNGLE

Harry asked for a map of China, we went to the library and found an Atlas. Harry turned to the page with the flags on. He looked along the flags in alphabetical order.

"Ah, this one says China 'Ch-i-n-a'. Now I can make my map. In China they have mountains as in India."

Approached reading area and spotted the giraffe and read the sign next to him 'I am lonely please read me a story' and sat down to share a book....

Phonics
Reading two-syllable words - read 'cool bag' by reading 'c-oo-l' 'cool' then 'b-a-g' 'bag' "Cool bag!"

'What's in the Box?' game. Reading cvc words and matching to pictures - read 'pig', 'net', 'dig' and 'pin'.

Matthew tried hard to read the words on the menu in the cafe role play area blending "ham" and "jam" on the sandwich menu.

Lauren had a bag and asked me to guess what was in the bag. I asked for a clue she said "I'll sound it out for you" P-U-P-I-T - its a puppet!!.

This is a m-u-d pie. Well its not chicken because it begins with m. He stopped and thought mud it say m-u-d.

Ty was reading The Gruffalo. He looked at the word Gruffalo & sounded out g-r-u-f it must be gruffalo!

Ty was reading independently, he sounded out 'mud', he looked at the picture and read 'mud.'

Sorting fiction and non-fiction books in continuous provision 'That's a non-fiction.... they have an video. That's got pretend pictures - it's a story book'

Listening to an adult read a Mr Men story. Commented 'Oh he's really angry now! It's not because he's nervous. He's angry because he let the dinghy go'

"There's a girl called Molly in this book, (laughs) that's my name".

When looking at Owl Babies Ty said O for owl, S for Sarah B for Bill. My Grandad is called Bill.

Matthew read a book about a café with complaining customers to 'Top Bear' in the reading corner. Matthew told him where to start "You start at the front not there!" He was able to blend CVC words. He blended: "This fish is too hot. This fish is not hot". "When will my fish come?". When asked: "Why do you think she's shouting where's my fish?!" He replied "She's hungry because she hasn't got any yet!"

Tom began by carefully selecting a book that we had read, telling me, "This is the one from last week isn't it!" He talked to himself as he carefully turned each page, sounding out phonically regular words on the first two pages – bus, pig, up and but, and locating tricky words – 'the' and 'said'. He continued to tell the story in his own words. He used many of the repeat phrases, "But **please** don't chat to the bus driver...."I won't." said the (correct animal) And he *did!*" He stressed the words and showed an awareness of audience. He talked through each page using picture clues and his previous knowledge about story pattern to support. Although I was there, he seemed for the most part to be reading the story to himself except at the end when he explained to me, "It's a funny book 'cos they did it when they said they wouldn't!"

Context

Mohsin is making a pizza and reading the instructions on the card.

Observation

Mohsin looked carefully at the instructions to make pizza as he constructed his own.

He read
'Put the ch....ee...s....e cheese on top. Put it in the o.. v..e.. n. oh its says oven. It sounds like a u!'

Later Mohsin used the photos of him making pizza and the instruction sentences to explain to the class reading each instruction as he did so.

Acts out story of 'Goldilocks and the three Bears' with two other children. He asked if he could use a squeaky voice to play the part of Baby Bear, stating 'I can do a really good squeaky voice!'

Context – Parental observation

Amber is at home with her mum. She reading her book and then goes and plays on her laptop

Observation

Amber has read all her book clearly and used different voices for speech as she reads it. she has also read the first page that the adult should read and only struggled with the word 'wrong'

She then decides to play on her learning laptop and was spelling simple words like cat, car, hat, fork completely independently sounding them out as she did so.

EYFS Profile exemplification for the level of learning and development expected at the end of the EYFS

Literacy

ELG10 – Writing

> Children use their phonic knowledge to write words in ways which match their spoken sounds. They also write some irregular common words. They write simple sentences which can be read by themselves and others. Some words are spelt correctly and others are phonetically plausible.

oh sataday I
Went to the
metrodoam
iswamandplaidwivsa
I Wenton the sild

Observation

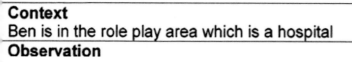

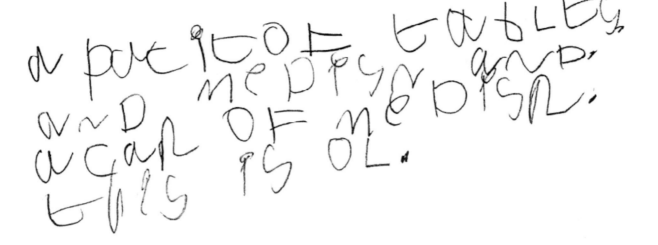

" a packet of tablets and medicine and a can of medicine. This is all".

Ben and Natalie were in the role play area. Natalie is pretending to be poorly. Ben writes out a prescription which will make her better he says.

'A packet of tablets and medicine and a can of medicine. This is all'

Oscar had spent over 40 minutes building a giant's castle with a small group. It was nearing the end of the session and he was keen that it was not taken down. "We need a notice now!" he announced, "I'm going to make it!" He organised himself in the writing area. This is what he wrote!

'Pleze doant BRak the casle' (Please don't break the castle)

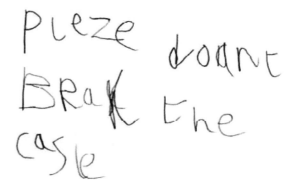

As he wrote he turned round to tell me, "This very important and special!" He proudly placed his notice on the castle and stood 'on guard.'

Jasmine.

I like droring at the droring tabl. I like to droring Flawe

And droring Hawsis. I am gud at dronin. Then I tid up and play awt.

Molly made a valentines day card for her mum and dad.

"I can spell 'happy', I've done it in birthday cards too - it's h, a, p, p, y – happy."

"valentines – hmmm – v, a, l, <u>val</u> e, n, <u>valen</u> t, i, n, s, s"

Context

Harry is on the Autistic spectrum continuum and has no speech.

Observation

Harry was observed writing the sentence below independently after singing the rhyme at group time. As he wrote he hummed to himself. After he had done this writing he went to the dressing up box, picked out some green fabric and draped it around his shoulders. He put on some red wellingtons and went outside where he jumped in the puddles

Frog is splash in the WATER

I went to Landa I sor dinosgor bons I went to the moysees m

Context

The class had been making card and there was a selection of resources in the mark making area. Scarlet chose to go to this area and independently wrote an invitation to Miss Swaine.

Observation

tomíss swayn

you ane inlited to my paty Love scarLett

Scarlet selected the paper and black felt pen. She copied 'invited' from a selection of helpful words. She wrote the key words independently – to, you, area, my and love and she used her phonic knowledge m-i-ss and s-w-ay-n.

She held the pen in her right hand with the correct pincer grip. She confidently wrote a, r, d, e – her letter m and n not so. When she had finished the card she took it to Miss Swaine with a big smile on her face as she read it.

'To Miss Swayn. You are invited to my party. Love Scarlett F xxxxxx'

Context
Set of instructions to how you get ready for 'Red nose' day – Aimee

Observation

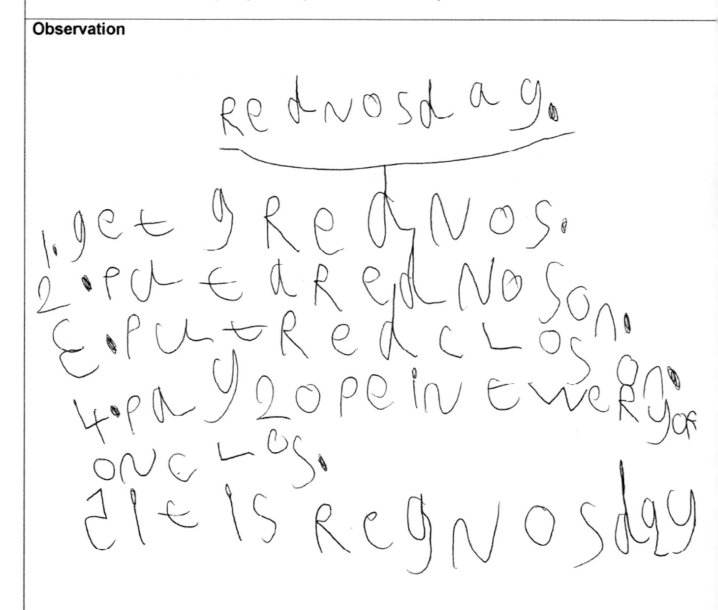

1. Get red nose. 2. Put your red nose on. 3. Put red clothes on. 4. Pay 20p in to wear your red nose. 5. It is red nose day!'

HOW TO Look avter mineebeest

1. dot stand on THem

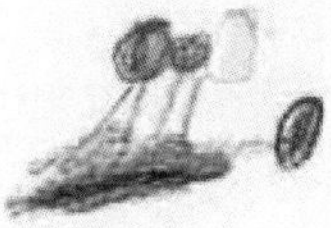

2. and nether Pik THem up

3. and nether CHas THem

4. Food and Frins Too

5. nether make hos Wen You make it School

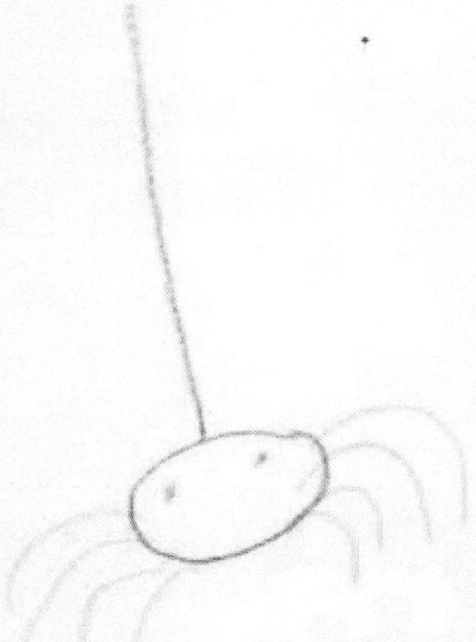

aht

Spider

caterpiller

bambee

Snayell

Ladybord

butrfliy

B excitedly explains all the components of his new quad bike. His friends listen and then begin to draw the bike and label the parts recalling the technical names of each.

Following this experience, B writes a letter to the teacher thanking her for letting him bring his bike to school.

His dad said, 'I've never seen him choose to write on his own like this before.'

After setting up an obstacle course, AL wrote, 'start', at the beginning of the course.

As dinosaur detectives, N. independently wrote a report on fossils for the dinosaur museum.

Mia

once a pona time
theh livd a boy
with his Mumy
ho tuc his cow
to the marcit
ho sar a od man
Whe galv the
Magic beens
Mums fraod thebees
a wai

The rich resources in the writing area inspired M to write her own version of the traditional tale, (from a previous story telling session).

M proudly tells the practitioner, 'I've written my own story, it's like the one in the book.'

WUDLOS   ANT

SID

Wym

ANT

ANT

Childminder's voice

After discovering an ant's nest whilst exploring in the garden, I offered D a magnifying glass which he was excited to use. D then decided to go on a mini beast hunt,

drawing and labelling, using phonic knowledge his discoveries in the garden.

Harry's most successful writing comes out of the continuous curriculum opportunities. He is keen to write notices that inform or instruct others as he sees these as important. "I'm writing this because everyone needs to know it!" On these occasions his body language indicates high levels of involvement. He reads this work back with expression.

He is showing a growing interest in writing and can now write his full name, some simple CVC and a few high frequency words. His letter formation is improving and the majority of letters are formed correctly. He uses his phonic knowledge to segment and spell simple words. When attempting to spell more complex words, is able to hear and write the initial and dominant sounds. He is beginning to write captions and simple sentences and is showing a greater understanding of the construction of a sentence. He is also developing left to right orientation.

To Harry I wish I cud red your books ro me

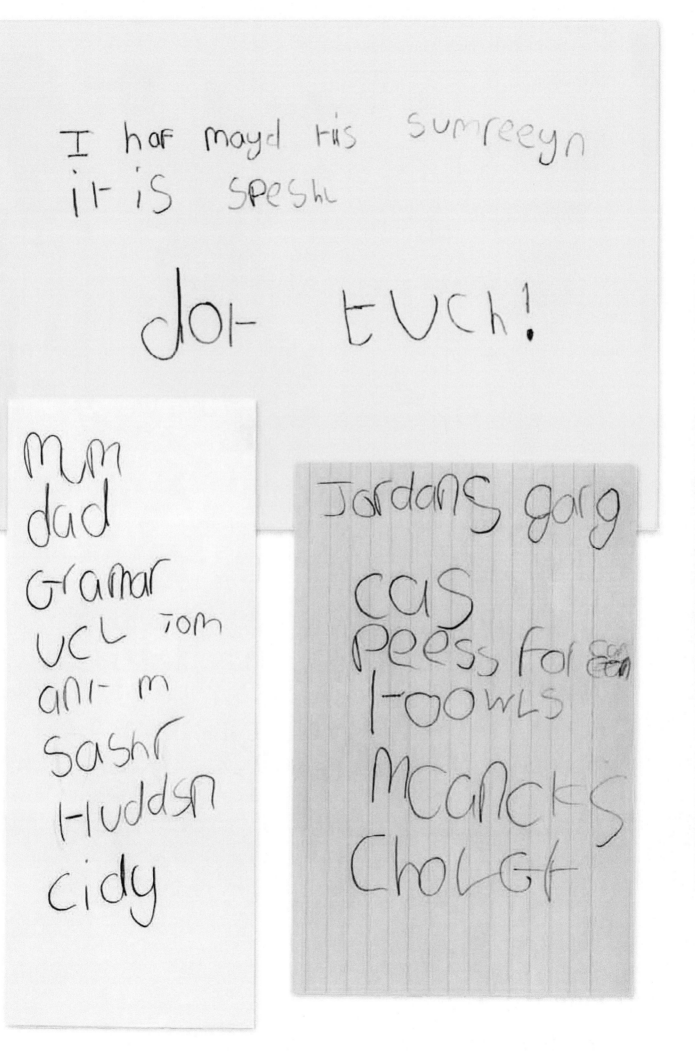

I haf mayd tiis sumreeyn
it is speshl

dot tuch!

mum
dad
Gramar
ucl Tom
ant m
sashr
Huddsn
cidy

Jordans garg
cas
peess for eem
toowls
Mcancks
cholct

Context
Set of instructions to how to plant seeds - Alfie

Observation

1 PUE SOiL iN POt
2 Put seeds in pot.
3. W aeer thepot

1. 'Put soil in the pot. 2 Put seeds in pot. 3. Water the pot'

To BLACbeard you are vere meen so itdinc you shood'dil poon Bear Bac so itdinc you shool worc the plane. From Dillan

Isobel

PLyoo hang up yor coat. DONt thom it on the fur.

EYFS Profile exemplification for the level of learning and development expected at the end of the EYFS

Mathematics

ELG11 – Numbers

Children count reliably with numbers from 1 to 20, place them in order and say which number is one more or one less than a given number. Using quantities and objects, they add and subtract two single-digit numbers and count on or back to find the answer. They solve problems, including doubling, halving and sharing.

J counted out 10 raisins. Then counted down as he ate them 10, 9, 8, 7, 6, 5, 4, 3, 2, 1.

'B' proudly showed a spider she had made.

"Oh no! It's got 7 legs now. One must have fallen off. I'm going to glue another leg so that it's got 8 again."

1 0 9 8 7 6 5 4 3 2

J wrote a countdown on his rocket! Well done ☺ This was done independently in The tree/writing area.

During a game of skittles outdoors Joseph knocked three numbered skittles down. He was able to calculate his score in his head. He added two and three together, the scores of the two smallest numbers together and then added five to the other five. He knew that he had scored ten in total. He also knew that this score had put him in the lead.

During a hunt for the dinosaur eggs Harry knew which number clue that he needed to find next. "You start at number 1, then you need to look for number 2, then number 3, then number 4 until you find all ten clues."

After finding a tub of conkers in the number resources, K. tipped them out into a builders tray and There are loads of them" She said she was going to "count them all to see how many there are altogether" When asked how many did she think there were she said that there was " ten hundreds"

She began to count each one place it in the bucket as she did. K accurately counted up to 30 conkers before getting lost in her counting. Once the bucket was full of conkers, she tipped them back into the tray and started counting again.

Ethan got most, he won.

Ethan got 7, Harry got 5

Ethan got 2 more than Harry.

Zachary and Anna had had quite a few throws which they had written down as a string of numbers or scores... (4 5 5 4 4) and (4 5 4 5 5) They soon realised it was too hard to add this many numbers together (we had been adding 2 scores together previously!) Anna got some compare bears and was sorting them into 'score piles'. They then used these piles to try and work out their total scores!

Context

Since joining the Foundation Stage Unit Christopher has demonstrated a real love for number. He thoroughly enjoys problem solving activities and readily engages in number challenges.

Christopher can confidently work with numbers to ten and beyond and he is able to apply this knowledge of numbers when completing simple addition and subtraction problems. He readily applies this knowledge in both the indoor and outdoor environment, for example whilst fishing in the water tray Christopher knew that if he took 2 fish away from the 8 fish in the water tray there would only be 6 left.

Christopher is developing a good knowledge of money and has enjoyed playing in the "local shop" especially when working behind the till! He is able to write a simple shopping list, identify cost, add amounts and identify the total amount using 1 and 2 pence coins. Christopher now needs to focus a little more on number formation as the numbers 2, 3, 7 and 9 can sometimes be reversed.

Observation:

During a registration Christopher was able to confidently answer how many children would be in the class if we had 1 more or 1 less. Also when asked how many children were away today and how many were left Christopher confidently replied "2 are away that leaves 27".

Observation: During child initiated activities Christopher was playing with the car mat. After sorting the different vehicle he was able to identify that he had 5 buses, 14 cars, 2 fire engines and 1 ambulance. When asked how many buses and fire engines he had altogether Christopher replied 7. He then touched and counted all vehicles and said " I have 22 altogether."

Childminder Voice

Whilst playing with the puzzles Christopher decided to touch and count all the pieces correctly 1,2,3,4...up to 24. Then taking one piece at a time and placing them into the puzzle he said " There are 24 if I put one back then I will have (he counted them again up to 23) 23." He repeated this process one by one until he reached 0 and all the pieces had been put into the puzzle. Christopher really enjoyed adding up all the pieces and putting them back one by one. He correctly counted the pieces back to zero. Christopher repeated this activity, when reaching 10 Christopher was able to identify one less for each number without using the puzzle pieces, stating the number and then counting the number of pieces left to check his own answers. Christopher was fully absorbed in what he was doing.

Observation:

At the self registration table Christopher identified that 6 children where staying at school for lunch, 6 children where staying for a packed lunch and 14 children where going home. Christopher said " Look Mrs Riley the packed lunches and the hot lunches are the same."

Observation: Christopher confidently place the number plates on the scooters and cars. He placed them in the correct order 1,2, 3, 4, 5, 6, 7, 8, 9, 10. With Kia and Ethan they matched the scooters and bikes to the correct parking spaces.

Observation: Christopher sorted the apples and the carrots stating "for snack time we have 17 apples and 14 carrots. There is more apples."

All About Me

When I am at school I am good at….

1. Counting my numbers. I can count to 22.

2. Solving tricky questions. "I like it when Mrs Riley asks how many packed lunch and hot lunches we have altogether ". "I also like it when she asks us which is more or less."

When I am at home I am good at …

1. Helping mummy when baking

2. Playing Mathletics on the computer

3. Playing snakes and ladders

What I would like to learn next….

1. Bigger numbers

What would my teacher like me to learn next?

1. To have a secure understanding of numbers to 20 and be able to apply this knowledge to a range of number problems in practical ways.

Observation: Whilst playing with the rocket ship Christopher confidently said "10, 9, 8, 7, 6, 5, 4, 3, 2, 1, 0 blast off."

Home / School links

Name: Christopher

Achievement : Christopher has been really interested in numbers all weekend. Whilst Out shopping we had to find the numbers 6 and 9. Every time Christopher spotted these numbers we had to stand still and freeze. At home Christopher enjoyed sequencing the numbers 1 - 20 independently.

Hannah made a chart of the children outside. She listed how many girls and how many boys were outside. Hannah was able to say that "There are 5 girls and 4 boys. That's 9 altogether".

G / B

5   4

Hannah.

Suzon...

Hannah.

Hannah counted her chart. "There are 15 children in and one child out. I have put a circle and a line because Brooke came in later".

Hannah made a chart. "This is circles for people who are out and lines for people who are in. It's a bit like a register but it's a chart". Hannah went around looking for children who were in class and who were outside.

Chloe was playing in the maths area. "I need three more" she said as she added some cubes to the circle. She then realised she had more than her friend. "Oh no, I have too many". She removed one. "Now we both have the same".

Cheri-May played basketball with another child. They decided to take it in turns and have 4 turns each. Cheri-May counted as her friend had a go – "My turn now, you've had 4!" she said.

Cheri-May enjoyed playing with the dominoes today. She matched the spots from one domino to the next, recognising the number straight away without having to count the spots. Well done Cheri-May!

Observation: When playing in the shop Christopher was able to use his shopping list to add 2 amounts. He said "the beans are 5 pence and the bananas are 3 pence, altogether that is 8 pence."

Hakima had chosen to collect all of the purple objects. She lined them all up and told me there were 16. She knew that 16 was a 1 and a 6. She could confidently tell me 1 and 2 more or less than 16, without counting, and she knew how to write each number.

Hakima was cutting fruit at the snack table. She chopped a banana into 5 pieces + put them into the bowl. She then cut another 4 pieces - "Now there are 9 pieces of banana!" she said.

Hakima was able to use the computer and smart board to play a maths game. Hakima had to count the spots then click on 'snap' if it matched the number, she got them all correct.

Hakima and her 3 friends went to work in the paint area. As they were sitting down Hakima looked at the chairs and said "We need another chair, we've only got 3!" She went and got another chair.

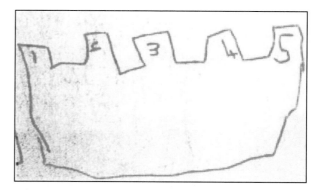

After looking at one more and one less when counting. Hakima drew this fantastic castle on the whiteboard with five turrets. She wrote the numbers 1-5, placing one number in each turret in order.

EYFS Profile exemplification for the level of learning and development expected at the end of the EYFS

Mathematics

ELG12 – Shape, space and measures

> Children use everyday language to talk about size, weight, capacity, position, distance, time and money to compare quantities and objects and to solve problems. They recognise, create and describe patterns. They explore characteristics of everyday objects and shapes and use mathematical language to describe them.

Edward was in the line waiting to go outside when he said; "I'm fourth!" Kamran misunderstood him and said; "I'm four!" Edward said; "He's not. Look!" and showed him what he meant by pointing to the children in the line and counting; "First, second, third, fourth – me. He's fifth!"

Kieron played with a ball outside. At one point he threw the ball over my head and said; "that went over your head, Miss Rayner!"

Gracie told me; "Not tomorrow, the day after… it's my birthday".

Monica and Cameron played in the pet shop together. Cameron said; "We need a 2p" and Monica picked up a 2p coin and said; "Here."

Ella and Thomas made a repeating pattern with the plastic bricks (an adult directed challenge). The tower also had to be taller than them. They worked well together…
Ella; "There you go Thomas" and passed him a brick.
Thomas; "Hang on – this one next".
Ella; "It's nearly taller than us!"
Ella; "It's going to fall over. It's getting taller than us".
Thomas; "One more! Hang on!"

When he had finished listening to 'The Giraffe who got in a Knot', Thomas correctly identified that the giraffe was "taller" at the end of the story (spontaneous comment), as he no longer had a knot in his neck.

Cameron was trying to pedal the taxi bike with a heavy passenger on the back. He said; "I can't do it with you, you're too heavy!"

Julia used the balance in the outdoor classroom. She put a large pebble in one of its buckets and placed pebbles in the other bucket until this side was lower than the other side. I said; "Oh look, that side has gone down. Why do you think that has happened?" Julia replied; "Because it's heavier."

Esme was making snail models with the dough. She said "the big piece will make a big snail. One is the littlest, one is the middle size one and this is the bigger one. The big one is heavy and the little one is light. One is large because I used lots of dough. The little one was lightest because I used a little bit of dough."

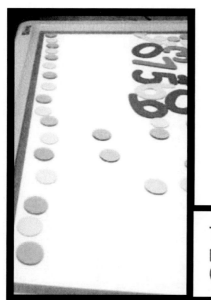

Euan made a sandcastle outside.
He put his spade through the middle of it and said; "that's half!".

Thomas made a repeating pattern on the light box (green, yellow, green, yellow).

Gracie was cutting out "circles". I asked her how she knew that what she was cutting out was a circle and she said; "it's got no corners."

Zak used the connecting camels and independently made a 'red, blue, red, blue' repeating pattern. Zak said to me; "Look at this – red, blue, red, blue... Now I try this one..." He then matched the connecting camels to the camels on the pattern card to make a 'blue, blue, orange, blue, blue, orange' repeating pattern.

2.11.10 AI Cheri-May enjoyed using the computer to create her own symmetrical pattern after seeing some Rangoli patterns. We were looking at how Hindus celebrate Diwali. She used the pointer to select colours and draw on the Smartboard. She said "Look at my pattern!" when she had finished.

Cheri-May made some fantastic repeating patterns on the smart-board today. She chose the shape and colour and decided what her pattern would be. Cheri-May correctly named all the colours and shapes and could tell me what would come next in each pattern.

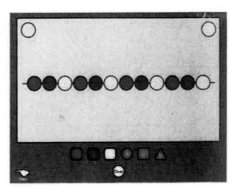

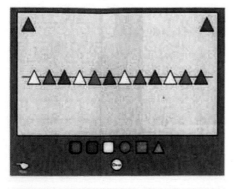

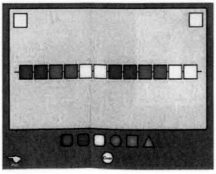

Cheri-may sorted the shapes into two groups. "The hexagons can all go together" She made another group with all different shapes in "Why are those all in that group, what have they all got thats the same?" I asked. "All of them have got four sides" Cheri-may said. Well done!

Cheri-May brought me this piece of paper and said "Look, I've done a hexagon." Cheri-May had drawn a hexagon over the lines of the hexagonal paper. "How do you know it's a hexagon?" I asked. "Because it's got 1, 2, 3, 4, 5, 6 sides." She pointed to each side as she said each number. Cheri-May went back to the writing area and drew some more hexagon shapes and then some different shapes inside the hexagons! Cheri-May named all the shapes – square, rectangle, circle, diamond and hexagon. Well done Cheri-May!

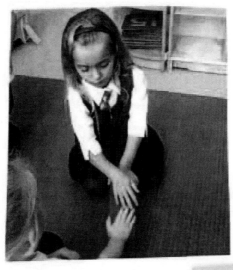

Cheri-May has been interested in colours and patterns today in the maths area.

She took the rainbow apart and then put it all back together. She used the words smallest, medium and biggest.

Cheri-May spent ten minutes exploring pattern and colour in the investigation area. She watched Matthew for a short while as he made a long pattern using beads. "That's good" Cheri-May said. She then selected some mirrored card and started to design her own pattern. Placing her beads carefully and purposefully

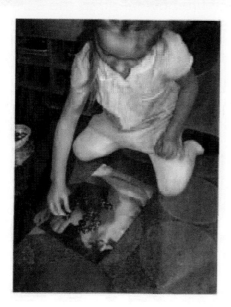

charlie keira x then
tristanoscan 5
Theo Marissasen 5
7 3
12

Charlie was playing with the cars outside, he was pushing them from across the other side of the ramp when he went off and found some chalk.

He came back and marked the playground where each car stopped. He then went and got a tape measure to measure how far apart the cars were.

He told Keira how far apart they were but she kept forgetting, so she suggested they wrote it down.

Once Keira was ready Charlie told her which number to copy from the tape measure onto her recording sheet.

He also pointed at the numbers so she was clear about which one to copy!

He correctly pointed to 5, 7, 3 and 12!

In the role play area Isobel counted how many coins she had.

I need to give the money to my friend. I've got ten pence.

I was building with some 3 D shapes.
"When the sphere is cut in half it has a flat side and a curved side. The flat side is a circle"
I decided to make some butterflies with the shapes in the office.
"I'm using a triangle for the bottom and two squares for the wings but I will turn them around so they look like diamonds".

Playing with 3D shapes

Making a shape butterfly

Alfred and Jacob were using cubes to make towers. They commented as they added more bricks that their tower was getting longer and longer. Jacob asked Alfred if he thought they could make it as tall as them. Alfred replied that they would need to go and find a few more cubes. They then discussed how tall they could make the tower if they added lots more bricks. 'We would need loads more it make it as tall as the ceiling', Jacob commented.

Kelise was working in the number area and she opened a drawer and found a large measuring tape.' Look we can find out how tall we are if we use this. We need to stand up against the board and we can check to see who is tall and who is short. My mummy has one of these on the door at home and we use it to see how much I have grown'

Ellie was working at the water tray and she knew that it would take 'quite a few' small bottles of water to fill the larger bottle she had in her hand.

Shaun was at the creative table making himself a headband. He had cut a length of paper and put it up around his head. When the ends wouldn't meet he commented that it was too short that he would need to get some more paper and add it on to the end. He cut himself a length of paper, stuck it on with sellotape and then re-measured it to check that it fitted. He then put his fingers on the right place and asked the adult to staple the ends together.

Observation:
Yahya says, "Mrs Philips, it's fantastic Friday today", as he comes into school first thing. "I'm going to see my aunty tomorrow, on Saturday."

Observation:
Engaged with class in shared story writing activity. Adult suggested children think of a time of day for the story. Yahya says "if it's early evening it could be six-eighteen p.m."

Observation:
Yahya is using the pointer stick, pointing to the weather chart. "Today is Friday 25th of November," he said to Mahdi who is standing next to him. "So yesterday was Thursday and tomorrow is Saturday. I'm going to see my aunty then. She helps me with my work, Mahdi."

Observation:
Yahya says "I've made a calendar, it's for my dad and I need to give it to his office so they know what number date it is."

A and J playing with conkers left in building tray. After playing with the conkers, tipping them into buckets and beginning to count them, A selected bucket scales which were made available and compared quantities in each of the buckets. He tried to explain that there were 'more conkers' in 'that bucket' because it went 'all the way down to the table.' He was able to identify which set of conkers were the heaviest.

Molly was working in the Chinese Restaurant role play area. Molly demonstrated her understanding and knowledge of money through her actions and use of appropriate language. She turned to the adult and said "Here's the bill. It's 50 pounds please." She had written the numeral 50 on a piece of paper. "Do you have enough money?" she asked The adult replied that she had a £50 note. "That's good" replied Molly "you won't need any change, that's exactly the right amount." She took the note and put it in the correct part of the till.

"Look at that aeroplane – it looks tiny but it's really very big! That's because it is so far away."

Desmond is working with Nadwah to weigh the animals using a balance beam/unifix. He counts carefully as N drops bricks into the pan up to 13.

There are too many bricks so Desmond suggests that they take two out. He selects two and removes them. He looks carefully at the balance beam to see if it is balanced. "It needs one more."

He is happy that it balances and counts the bricks to 12 accurately. He has a different animal and predicts that it will be heavier than N's.

He carefully drops bricks into the pan, watching closely until he is happy. He counts bricks to 14, but stops counting to concentrate on looking.

L   conversation

L is outside involved in child-initiated learning in the sand tray. Within the tray are collections of natural materials - leaves, pebbles, conkers, sand and a selection of containers.

The practitioner observed and noted . . . .

" you got to sort these out " (said L)

" put all the same, they're all lumpy " (L feels the bumps on the pebbles)

" This is the thickest one. Now I'm finding conkers - there's one, I missed it. I think I might see one again. It's a tiny conker "

(After collecting the conkers, L counted them carefully, 1, 2, 3, 4, 5, 6. L then found 2 pine cones and said,

" this is the tiny one, this is the big one, it's the prickiest one, this one is smooth ".

Emma and Leo are playing in the rockpool.

They talk about how heavy the rocks are.

Emma adds more to her net. "Now it's extremely heavy" she says, then adds another, "it's even heavier now!"

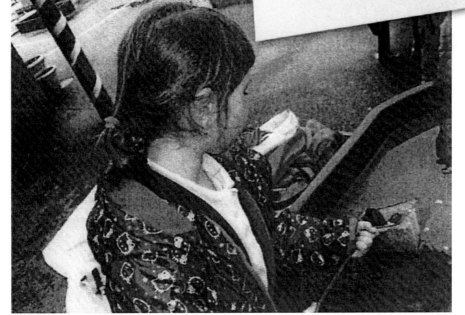

James built some towers with the wooden blocks.

"That's even bigger" he said, "it's enormous!"

When discussing dinosaurs James said "the one with the longest neck is the tallest."

Outdoor robot theme.

Self initiated activity in outdoor area exploring old computer parts. Selected measuring tape and said, "the keyboard is 23 centimeters."

A Reception child using a tape measure to measure an old keyboard.

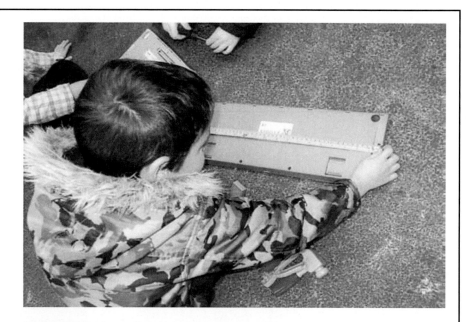

Hannah and Honey were playing in the shop. They used the language of capacity, full empty, half full, to talk about how full the bottles were. They were able to place the bottles in order starting with the fullest.

Ben had been throwing snowballs at the wall. He was excited as he managed to get them higher and higher up the side of the building. 'Look that one's gone really high, it's nearly touched the top of the window. If I throw a bit harder then I can make it go even higher. It might be as tall as a giant'.

Name: O	Date:

Observation & context:

O compared his foot
to the footprint found on
the bridge.
"Mrs. Mutchell it can't
be my foot. look it's
too small".
Oliver then went on to
measure his foot using
multilink cubes and
found it was 10 cubes long.

Child / ~~adult~~ initiated

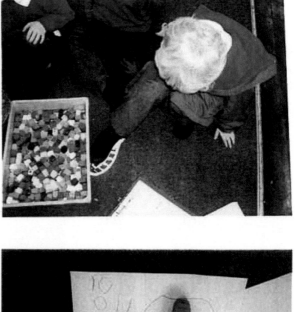

There was a giant footprint found
in class after the children had
heard & enacted the story of the
3 Billy Goats Gruff. The question was
posed "Who's footprint is this?"

Observation & context:

These children were fascinated by the new
wooden marble run. They spent a long
period of time engaged in a complex
problem solving activity as they tried to
work out how to build a structure which
would allow a marble to pass freely from
one end to another. They all worked
harmoniously throughout, allowing each
other to improve their construction or
otherwise as they explored different
combinations.

"Let put this long bit here,
the marble goes faster

Child initiated

then"

O selected unifix cubes
to measure his footprint. He
carefully fitted the bricks
inside the outline he had
drawn & added 2 more
bricks until the column was
the right length. He accurately
counted 10 bricks. "Mine is
10 long, he shouted excitedly!

Can you hang
my bird feeder
really high for the
birds.

Name: _____ **Date:** _____

Observation & context:

The boys were investigating sinking and floating in the water tray. ____ had place a bowl in the tray and commented that it floated and noted that it continued to float as he added water but. "If I fill it up it will not float".

____ then got a sponge and began squeezing water in. He wanted to add as much water as he could "Just enough but not enough to sink it."

"I think this will be just enough".

Harry had put a sponge in the water and was watching it carefully. "This is filling up with water but its still

Child / ~~adult~~ initiated

Observation & context:

not sinking. It's floaty."
They then worked together to put water in using the pipes.
S "we're trying to make it sink now".
R "oh the pipes not going down the right way — the water won't go this way" — as

Rocket made in the office.

"My rocket can go up, up, up higher than the moon"

Name: _____ **Date:** _____

Context: Construction   **AL PSRN**

~~Adult-directed~~ / child initiated

Observation

____ was building a very tall 'truck'. As he built it higher it started to wobble. 'oh no! its falling'. He looked carefully and then said 'I can fix it' He then spent a lot of time working out how he could build it higher without it falling.

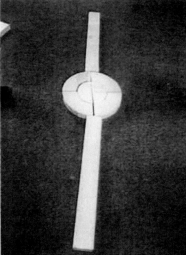

O ____ made this 'watch' with bricks. He carefully searched for the appropriate bricks from the shelves to complete the circles. Each brick he found was the 'right' one to fit in next. "Its a Ben 10 watch" he said. "Its a circle"

"My pattern is grey, white, black, grey, white, black." "white, black."

Name: O
Context Outdoor Area.

Observation
O was working with other children in a shop they had created outside. He was writing number sentence "....because you have to add up to know what it costs."

I helped my dad put together a flat-pack side board. We had to match numbers and letters to fix the pieces together and Dad let me have a turn at fixing them together with a big hammer.

O

Name: O
Context: Maths area

Observation:
O   has been very interested in the scales and weighing different objects . Today he was at the table weighing numerous things, putting them in the scales, taking them out and watching the movement of the scales carefully. He put one animal on one side and picked up another. 'Can you tell me which is the heaviest?' I asked. ' This one is, it goes down.' he replied, and later, 'This one has got three big animal in so this is the heaviest.' He pointed to the side of the scales touching the table.

"Like we learned this morning but snakes; small, medium, large. Pointing at circles."

While my neighbours were on holiday, I looked after their 2 rabbits, Stanley and Gladys.
I fed them dry food on a morning and vegetables on an evening.
O

"Can I make one too?" O chose to make a necklace from multicoloured straw beads threaded onto thin wire. "I'm going to start with black....... .... and do a pattern, pink, black pink black." After a while he said. "I'm changing now I'm going to make it multicoloured." "Look there's a bit from a pasta jar ...... I've got toads on mine."

"I've made the moon. It shines in the sky at night."

E is very interested in patterns of squares. Here she has drawn a picture of 'Little Lumpty's' Wall. Each square she has coloured has a yellow border & orange centre. Later in the month she used a similar design to make a pattern with white stones. Again the outer borders of each square are made up of small white stones, with one larger white stone in the centre of each square.

A repeating pattern.

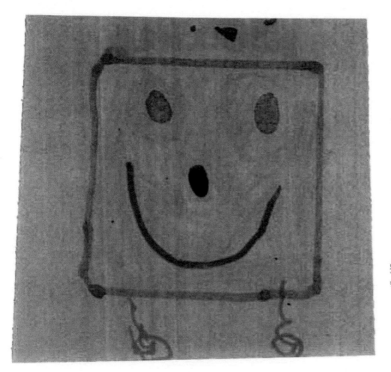

Observation

E chose to work in The writing area. She selected various squares & drew round them to make 'shape monsters'. She could describe some of the properties of the square, "It has 4 corners and 4 sides.

E regularly chooses to work in the construction area with the Community Playthings bricks. She often builds walls selecting different lengths of bricks but making the ends of the bricks line up together. She has a clear idea of which bricks to select for complete each layer. E will often arrange small world people along the top of the wall when it is completed & play for 10-15 mins alongside & with other children imagining scenarios for these characters.

Hakima was busy playing with the sorting objects today. She began making a pattern of purple and blue objects in a circle. Hakima then did another pattern of orange and yellow objects inside the circle. She repeated this with three more circles of repeated colour patterns, carefully placing the objects in the right position.

Hakima made these super repeating patterns on the whiteboard outside today. She chose the pens carefully to make sure her pattern stayed the same. Well done Hakima!

Hakima built a complex model with the wooden jewel blocks. She chose each block carefully, selecting the correct size blocks to fill in any gaps. She then chose an arch shaped block "I need this curved one for my bridge."

on top

in front

in

under

next to

AI Hakima did some super position work today. She had to choose where to place the teddy bears in the garden and then tell me where she had put them using position words. Hakima then matched the label to where each teddy was by sounding out the words. Well done Hakima!

Hakima was painting and went to choose a new piece of paper. She paused and said "Hmm. I think I'll do a square pattern" - she chose the square piece of paper + painted a series of squares inside each other.

Hakima followed some tricky instructions today using positional language. I asked Hakima to put the objects in different places. She correctly put Mr. Alien in the basket, the ball inbetween the chair and the basket, the ribbon on the chair and the blue fabric in front of the basket. She also knew what behind and under meant. Well done Hakima!

After collecting twigs, children use plasticine to make shapes. They discuss the properties of shapes with the practitioner.

"Look, I have made a triangle with three twigs. It's got three corners."

Practical maths – here C seperates keys between two doors and proudly uses a whiteboard to record the number sequence.

Outdoors, the practitioner uses a practical context which engages the children's interests to inspire them to count.

Here a group of children take part in a traffic survey, excitedly discussing and recording how many of each type of vehicle they had seen, comparing quantities.

Children engage in making 'moveable arty pictures', here G decides to use the different types of pasta to make a repeated pattern. She describes the pattern to her friend who then attempts to recreate it.

After an adult led activity outdoors, a group of children consolidate and extend their knowledge by exploring the capacity of a range of containers, talking about which will hold the most/least and comparing qualities.

J: "Mine is fuller than yours."

B: "If I pour two pots in the jug it is full."

EYFS Profile exemplification for the level of learning and development expected at the end of the EYFS

Understanding the world

ELG13 – People and communities

> **Children talk about past and present events in their own lives and in the lives of family members. They know that other children don't always enjoy the same things, and are sensitive to this. They know about similarities and differences between themselves and others, and among families, communities and traditions.**

A: "They're asleep. My baby's grown up, she's 4."

P: "My baby's only little. She's 1. How old is your baby L?

L: "She's 8. My sister's 8."

P: "But my sister's bigger. She's called Sophie".

L:"I'm going to put her to sleep in the cot".

S: "Put her there."

L: "She's heavy." *L puts the baby's toys and bottles next to the baby.*

S: "Put the bottle there". *S points to the cot pillow……*

L: "She wants some dinner ".

Pr: "What does she want?"

L: "She wants custard. Like that baby up there." *S points to a baby photo on the wall*

"That's me a long, long time ago. I was two."

L collects a knife, fork, spoon and dish.

L speaks to the baby "I'll cut it up". *She stirs the food in the dish and continues to feed the baby as she speaks to S.*

"Look there's S". *She points to S's baby photo on the wall as she continues to feed the baby.*

"One more, no two more, no four more, 1,2,3,4". *L accurately counts as she feeds the baby.*

Pr: "Do you need help to get her wind up?". *L nods and the Practitioners demonstrates how to wind the baby. L copies the action.*

"Oh yes they burp and then you have to put them to bed."

19.01.10 Julia and Gracie are playing 'schools' in the 'office' role play area.
1:25
Julia is pretending to be a teacher taking the register. She makes ticks on a piece of paper after calling out different children's names. Gracie answers her and whispers suggestions for different names.
Julia; "Good morning, Julia... Good morning" and giggles. "I like it more when people call me 'Sisi', my Poland name." She comes to the window of the role play area and says to me; "Can I be Sisi, Mrs Carlier? I like it more."
Julia counts the ticks on her 'register' and says; "Our class is twenty... No, eleven."
Julia; "Pretend everybody Polish. To be Polish you have to come from Poland."
Gracie; "Say things in Polish. Do your name in Poland."
Julia; "I will show you how to write my name in Poland."
1:31
Julia; "My name is 'Sisi' – it starts with a 'S' [sound]." She begins to do the register again and the girls giggle when they say 'nonsense' names. Julia counts "twenty-four" ticks. Julia begins to do a dinner register and asks me what to write for packed lunches. I say "'s' [sound] for sandwiches."
Gracie asks; "Is 'hot school dinners' a 'h' [sound]?"
1:35
Gracie and Julia write down numbers and ask me what numbers they have written. Gracie's number is eleven million, two hundred and seventeen thousand, three hundred and eight. Julia wrote three hundred and twenty-seven thousand.
Gracie said; "That's smaller than mine."
Gracie; (Looking at the clock) "It's time to go home – you have to ring the tambourine."
(L.C.)

29.04.10 Euan came up to me and said; "Guess what, Mrs Carlier – this is exciting! I've got new socks because I'm getting holes in my socks like my brother." Child initiated (L.C.)

11.09.09 Cameron told me that his Mummy was going to a hotel for two nights and that because of this he was going to his Nanny's for two nights (child initiated). S.R.

When talking about Christmas Amelia said "I have to wait to open my presents til after dinner". Ben said "that must be hard Amelia". Amelia replied "its cause my Daddy is a fireman and he has to go to work and he would be sad if we opened them and he wasn't there." Ben said "that is kind. We open ours in the morning."

Ben said "when I went to George's house we had to play in the toy room and not in the living room like in my house."

Context

Finlay joined the school at the beginning of F1. Before starting at the school he spent three days a week with a local childminder. He is collected by the childminder two days per week. The childminder has close links with the school and is keen to extend children's experiences during sessions in her care.

Finlay is an only child but has a large extended family with cousins in the school. He spends a lot of time with his wider family and often has lots to say about times when they have all been together at the weekends or during the holidays.

As his father travel a lot with work Finlay is often keen to talk about places his dad has been to.

Finlay has a large group of friends and gets on well with other children. He is always willing to offer help to both adults and children. He enjoys talking about the things he has done at home.

Finlay is a member of the local Beaver group and goes to the out-of-school football club.

Observation during child-initiated play

Finlay and Oliver are sitting in the book area looking at books and talking about the pictures. Finlay says "There's a big dog in my book, he's going to bite the mister." He turns to Oliver and says "My dad got bit by a dog once when he was little. He had to go to the hospital and have an injection."

Incidental observations

At the snack table Finlay says "I'm going to save this apple for Kira because she doesn't like oranges."

Observation during child-initiated play

Whilst playing in the home corner Finlay picks up the takeaway menus. "I don't like Indian food like daddy does. I tried it but it was too spicy. I like Chinese noodles like mummy!"

Context - Large group morning circle time session.

During circle time Finlay was keen to tell the rest of the group about his Uncle Dan's visit from America. "My Uncle Dan is staying at my house. He is from America. It took him 10 hours to get here on an aeroplane. When I am bigger he said I can go and stay at his house. Mummy won't want to come though because she doesn't like going on aeroplanes."

Parent voice

Home/school diary entry - On Saturday Finlay made a birthday card for Granny's 60th birthday. He took it to her party on Sunday. She was really pleased with it!

Conversation with parents at the beginning of the day-
"Fin had a great time at Beavers last night. They had a Chinese New Year party. They were all doing Chinese dragon dancing and Fin was at the front as the head of the dragon. He was really good at it."

Fin took part in the Remembrance Day parade with Beavers.

Hearing Dogs

During a visit from Mr Perry and Alfie his hearing dog, Finlay was keen to ask questions and inquisitive about what it must be like to be deaf. He asked Mr Perry "What does Alfie do when the door bell rings?" and wanted to know how the dog helped deaf people cross the road.

A few days later, whilst sitting with Miss Metcalf, Finlay said "I think Alfie is a really clever doggy. It must be horrible when your ears don't work properly."

India Day

As part of the school 'India Day' Finlay took part in a range of topic related activities. He chose to dress up in traditional Indian dress in the role play area and played alongside others to prepare Indian food for his 'family' and friends who played alongside him.

Finlay used the CD player to play Indian music and used the musical instruments in rhythm to the music. Finlay and Oliver danced to the music copying some of the movements the dancers had shown them during the dance workshop earlier in the week.

Finlay was keen to take part in the cooking activity. He was able to use a range of kitchen utensils to grate and chop the ingredients. He used the knife safely and followed the instructions given to him. Finlay was willing to try the chickpea curry even though he said he didn't like the smell of the finished dish. When he tried a small spoonful he said "I don't like it, the chickpeas are a bit mushy!"

Context– Whole group 'show and tell session'

Finlay brought to school his collection of coins. He explained to the class about how his dad travels with work and often brings back coins for his collection. "This is American money. Daddy told me that they use dollars in America. This is a Euro. We had to spend these when we went on holiday last year"

Childminder voice

Finlay spent two days with his childminder during the half term holiday. Staff discussed some of the activities Finlay had taken part in during this time.

"Finlay had been excited to tell us all about going to see the fireworks after leaving me on Thursday. Because he was so excited we spent the day making firework pictures, using the instruments to make firework sounds for the younger children. He was a bit worried that the really loud bangs might frighten the babies! Finlay was keen to use exciting words to describe the sounds of different fireworks. He also spent quite a long time with Joe (one of the older children) on the computer finding out information about Guy Fawkes. He was fascinated by the Houses of Parliament cellars!"

B drew his family and said "This is my Dad, but he doesn't live at my house. I do like it when I can go and stay with him"

L knew that a baby horse was called a foal. He talked about the horses his family had at the travellers' site.

"I like to see me playing outside with my sister. I can't remember some of the things I did!"

"I was walking around at the fair..I have to walk with my mam..L has to walk too..just walk..L and me are cousins. We are gypsy..My brother is B. He's little"

L describes his Mammy's favourite colour

"She likes dark blue the best".

Context: children recorded their favourite things at home and then discussed it with their key worker.

"My favourite toy is a kitten..Mommy bought me a fluffy kitten when I came home from hospital..when I was born."

"My favourite TV programme is Simpsons...We both snuggle and watch Simpsons after we've had our tea."

"I have moved into a house now - I used to be in a trailer on the site"

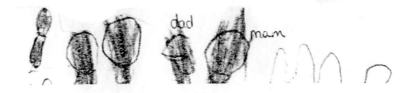

Celebrations

Context: During Circle Time there had been a discussion about the different festivals celebrated by children. Children made the following comments after a circle time discussion.

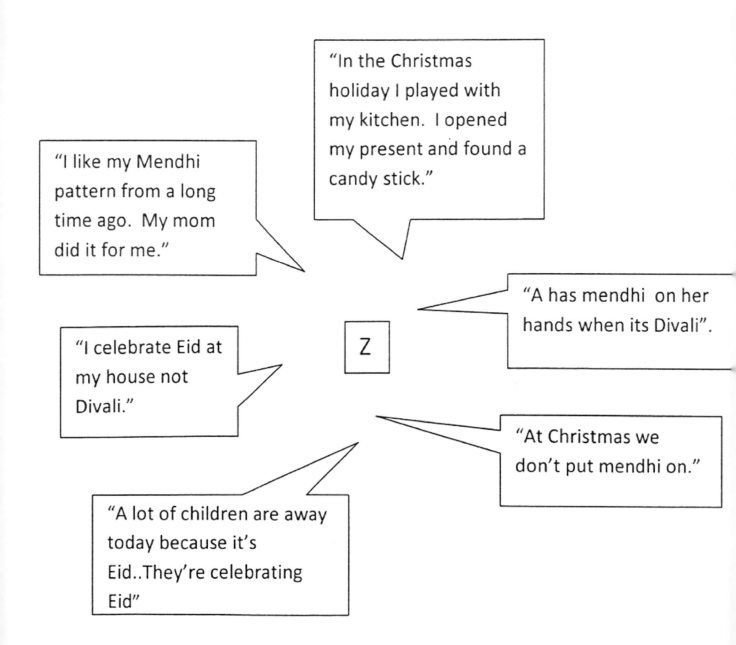

"In the Christmas holiday I played with my kitchen. I opened my present and found a candy stick."

"I like my Mendhi pattern from a long time ago. My mom did it for me."

"A has mendhi on her hands when its Divali".

Z

"I celebrate Eid at my house not Divali."

"At Christmas we don't put mendhi on."

"A lot of children are away today because it's Eid..They're celebrating Eid"

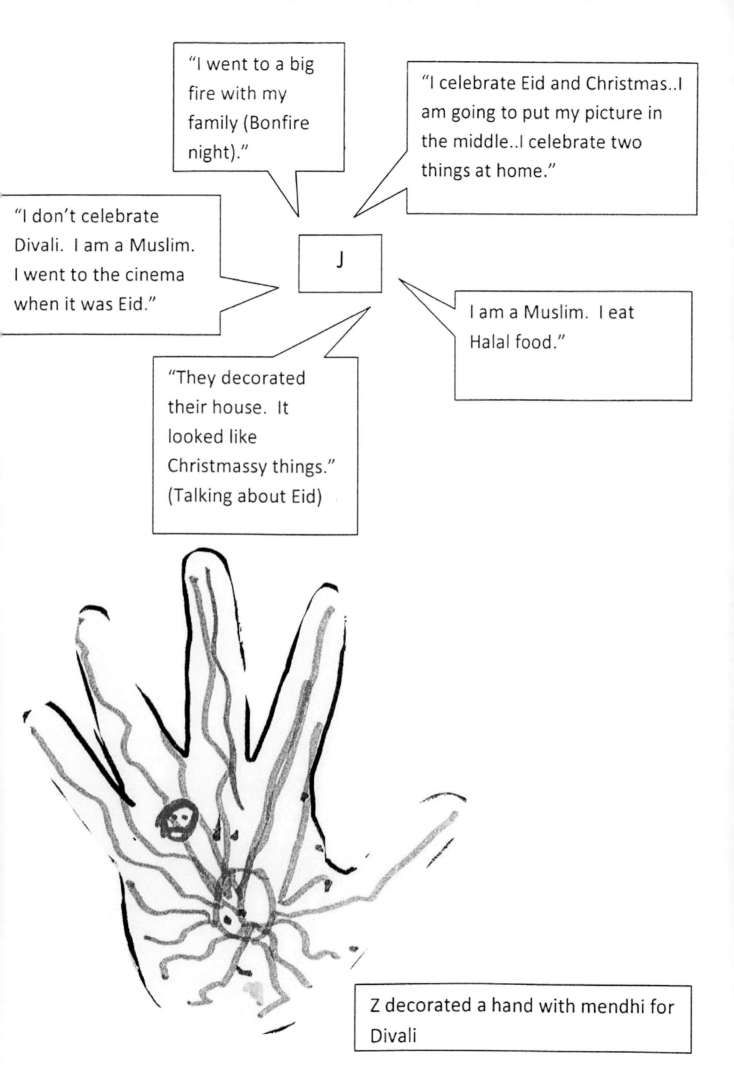

"I went to a big fire with my family (Bonfire night)."

"I celebrate Eid and Christmas..I am going to put my picture in the middle..I celebrate two things at home."

"I don't celebrate Divali. I am a Muslim. I went to the cinema when it was Eid."

J

I am a Muslim. I eat Halal food."

"They decorated their house. It looked like Christmassy things." (Talking about Eid)

Z decorated a hand with mendhi for Divali

KA talked to the whole class about Christmas at home. Her family are from Germany.

" We put out shoes – all of us and we get presents from the saint. "

Later, at snack time she talked about going to Germany to visit family.

" I have to have a passport. Do you have a passport ? (To her friend CH)

cnd take turns at the end of the day to choose and sing their favourite nursery rhyme in front of the class. MA chose to sing a song in Polish. We were very surprised – the song is about a cucumber! She told us that she learnt the song at the Polish school she attends on Saturdays.

During circle time, CA told the group about his weekend in Skegness with his Nan & Grandad. They went fishing.

DI used chalk outside to draw a picture of his family at a firework show. "The park was massive! I got really scared so my Dad held my hand."

Date: Time: 2.15pm   By: GW
Context: In classroom, teacher, JA and LU.
Both boys were talking about football and started to argue about which team was the best.
Adult: "LU loves Italian football and supports an Italian team. JA loves football here in England. "
Both boys nodded and agreed. Carried on playing then went outside to play football. Played for 15 minutes, came inside and announced together that Italy and England drew. Laughed.

MA's mum, We went to church yesterday. She loves to go as we sing lots and she spends time with me and her Daddy, She asked why lots of people have blue eyes when she has brown eyes. This led to a lovely discussion about where people are from

Alex made and tasted pea soup. Alex said it tasted better than the soup he made at Nursery

Name: AR	Date:	By: LW

Context and content of observation:
Eid Party
AR   We made Pakoras for Eid, me and my mummy made them this morning. We are Muslim and we have a party and wear pretty dresses like this one. It is very beautiful, do you like it? I have to be careful so I don't get it dirty.

JO : Yum! I've had these before at my home when we have Chinese takeaway. They're really nice!

ET : I do, I love these crisps.

DA : I don't like anything!

JO : They're prawn crackers, not crisps. Try one!"

DA : Nope. Don't like them. (After tasting).

JO : (claps his hands). Well done for trying! I'll have them with ET, yeah?

ET : Yeah!

My Baby Album

Here is Eden giving the baby a bath. Eden undressed the baby, checked the water temperature by testing the water with a bent elbow. He then squeezed some bubbles into the water and mixed them with his hand. Eden used the sponge to wash the baby.

Whilst bathing the baby, Eden told me all about his new baby brother and how he helps his Mummy bath him.

Eden finished washing the baby and then unfolded the towel and placed it over the end of the water area.

When looking at a baby photograph of M's friend commented 'She looks tiny there, and now she has grown. She had dark brown hair like mine, now she has blonde hair'.

In the role play area M said 'We are going to try on our dresses today because my aunty is getting married. The boys can't see how pretty we are so they have to wait downstairs. She is getting married at a church far away'.

M visits her caravan each weekend in Bournmouth. She talks enthusiastically about going on the beach and taking sun cream.

My house is in (village name)

I've got a bath with jets in . You press the button and it all shoots out.

On village walk stated 'I like the houses, but it's very smelly in some places'.

It's my idea to make a church. I've put a candle for the prayers.

M recalled events from her holiday.

She explained that a seal had been washed up on the beach. She also described the jelly fish (It had tentacles).

EYFS Profile exemplification for the level of learning and development expected at the end of the EYFS

Understanding the world

ELG14 – The world

> **Children know about similarities and differences in relation to places, objects, materials and living things. They talk about the features of their own immediate environment and how environments might vary from one another. They make observations of animals and plants and explain why some things occur, and talk about changes.**

'B' helped to harvest the potatoes.

She was fascinated to find potatoes amongst the roots:

"These are roots. It's like hair that stays in the mud and keep it still. They drinked the water to get big. I didn't think they would be red."

"We're gonna cook them up in water 'cos chips give you a big tummy. Chips are potatoes and bad to eat all the time."

Frozen Sea Creatures

Context: After a cold night, the children discovered that the outdoor water tray had frozen. The children are amazed to see that animals and sea creatures are stuck inside the ice.

During the observation, a small group of boys discuss and investigate how to 'free' the trapped sea creatures and animals.   Duration: 20 minutes+

The group peer at the frozen surface and touch it with their hands. Child C taps it with his knuckles. Child L taps it with a toy hammer.

C: "We need to melt the animals out".

L "We need to warm them up..that will melt the ice."

The group discuss different ways to 'warm them up'

L: "We can blow them warm."

Child L blows on the ice and other children join in for several minutes.

C: "It's not working...Look the sun is coming out. The sun is hot. It can melt the ice."

The group work together to move the frozen water tray into the sunshine. They return several times during the session to see if the ice is melting. When it eventually melts, they excitedly 'rescue' the animals.

Context
Oliver is digging in the growing box outside

Observation
Oliver is digging in the growing box during outdoor provision. He is digging a hole using the spade and the fork. I am planting herbs here'. Oliver digs one of the last year's herbs out of the box. 'Look its dying can you see the roots?.... can I have the watering can because it needs water' He waters the herb and then says 'It will grow now it's had some water' He continues to make more holes to put herbs in

Context – Parental contribution
Amber and I are sat looking at a science book

Observation
Amber said 'Mummy, the great white shark is the biggest shark that sometimes eats people and the blue whale is the biggest mammal and that mammals have to have warm blood and a spine'. She showed me where her spine was (along with her heart, lungs, and brain!)

Context – Parental contribution
Amber is sat I the car. We are driving to the zoo.

Observation
'Mummy, when the sun is up and we're awake, the moon is up and people are asleep on the other side of the world and when the moon is up and we're asleep here, people on the other side of the world are awake and the sun is up'

- "I like the park. I find conkers from the tree. There's sometimes conkers ready....when they fall they are ready".

- ------- made a house on the interactive white board. 'My house is joined to other houses. I live at no 110 my friend ___ lives next door. My door is white and her door is blue, so I did white and blue. My house is first because it is the oldest'.

- When handling fish a child commented" The octopus feels soft, gooey and squidgy. The fish feels hard and smooth. Is this the eye of the mackerel?

- Out in the playground one child to another child. 'Can you hear that chirping sound? It's a robin because it's got a red tummy. It's in that bush (pointing).'

- 'I'm not every going to touch the octopus it's slimely. She noticed the slits on its tummy. ' It's been cut by a sharp rock she told me.

- 'The sun is making the ice melt because the sun is hot and the ice is cold. It melts because it gets warm.'

- 'Electricity makes everything work in the classroom. It's kind of ... you know the plug, electricity comes from those plug things into the room. Electricity is in the wire.'

- 'When you push down the spring it jumps up.'

"It's squashy, but then it gets hot and it's hard and delicious!"

William chose to experiment with the magnets. He enjoyed finding out which objects would be attracted to the different types of magnets on offer. 'Horse shoe magnets are stronger than any other magnet,' he said confidently 'I've tested them all and it's harder to pull things off that one!'

He carefully studies the broad bean seed which had just started to sprout. 'I am amazed the root didn't come from this black bit on the bean ... I thought it would... that's why we do experiments to see if what we think happens!' said William.

Hannah re-erected the visit to the woods. She gathered a range of materials, plants and objects to represent the woods

She then drew a picture of the frog pond and her friends around the frog pond. Hannah pointed out the frog spawn which will turn into frogs

Gracie and Monica looked at the things that I had frozen in blocks of ice. Gracie asked lots of questions about how I had made them and how the objects had "got inside". She described the ice as "slippy" and saw how blocks of ice slipped off when she placed them on other blocks of ice. She predicted that the smallest block of ice would melt first and recognised that her fingers were making the ice melt as she touched it.

Finlay came up to me with a clear yoghurt pot and said; "do you think this will float with a car in it?" I explained what I thought would happen and asked Finlay how we could find out. Finlay said; "test it." The water tray was outside and so Finlay went outside to test the yoghurt pot 'ferry'. He came back in to me after a short time and told me that the yoghurt pot floated when by itself. When the car was inside Finlay said; "it sorts of floats and sort of sinks." He explained that the yoghurt pot floated initially but then filled with water and sank. He speculated that this was because the car was too heavy. He decided to see if the yoghurt pot would remain floating if he put some lighter objects inside. He tried it with a playmobil man and then a glass nugget and it floated. He continued to experiment with different objects for the rest of the afternoon.

When Aiden was making a pond in the creative area he said, "let's put frogs in the pond and let's put tadpoles in the pond cause you don't get one without the other."

When Finlay was taking part in an adult-led activity to look at hen, duck and quail eggs, Finlay said; "they [the chickens] have to sit on the eggs to keep them warm – like a radiator". He also said; "eggs are different colours. Ostrich eggs are big and spotty".

When making egg sandwiches as part of a small group, Finlay commented on the differences between raw and cooked eggs; "the 'jelly' has turned white. The white bit isn't runny. The yolk isn't runny either".

On a welly walk around the school grounds. Gracie spotted a lavender bush and said; "that's lavender. I like the smell".

Cameron pointed to some mushrooms growing outside and asked; "What are they?" Harriet answered; "They're mushrooms. You can't eat them. They may be poisonous."

Jaden, Harriet, Monica and Poppy looked at the things we had put up from our 'Windy Day' box. Some of the comments they made are as follows;
Poppy; "Look at these Jaden [the wind chimes]. It makes a nice song".
Harriet; "When the wind blows it bangs on the wood".
Monica; "The wind makes it look like it's going up and down".
Jaden; "It goes up and down".

Following a trip to Farmer Nick's farm in Wrington, Harry said; "I liked the hares because they could run really fast. They are bigger than rabbits. They have long ears"

Jaden, Euan and Thomas used the guttering to shoot the cars up into the air today (instead of down). At one point Jaden said; "We have to shoot them up fast!"

Before a trip to Farmer Nick's farm in Wrington, we asked the children what they thought they would see. Abi said; "Lots of animals like muddy pigs and some cows being milked".

Finlay used a drainpipe and ball and experimented with how best to roll the ball down the pipe. He worked out that if he leant the drainpipe up against the fence and went the other side he could pop the ball in easily.

Finlay showed me a caterpillar he had spotted on a leaf in our outside classroom. I said; "I wonder what kind of butterfly it will turn into" and Finlay replied that he thought it would become one that looked like the caterpillar.

Context: Forest School afternoon

Jack and Anna worked together to build the den. Jack asked Anna to get some string. They held it and cut it together. They were talking to each other as they worked. "This makes the den stronger" said Jack They asked the teacher to tie the knot. (…. talks about the features of making a den strong)

Georgina and Darcie carried the big log to the den. They knew they had to work together because it was so heavy. "This is the seat "said Darcie "because it is big". "Our den has a seat" she shouted to the class, Together they decided to put it at the side of the den.

The Green dragon

Hannah had been to the woods with the rest of the class. Whilst they were in the woods they heard the story of the Green Wizard who looks after the animals who live there.

In the woods Hannah used the lego digital camera to record the events in the story.

In the small world area, Hannah created a woods environment and gathered small world forest animals. She made a nest for the owl, a hole for the rabbit and talked to the teacher about the places the animals chose to live. Hannah talked about camouflage and how the animals can hide in the woods.

Hannah then decided to write the story of the Green wizard using 2creste a story.

The Frog Pond

After a walk around the school grounds and a visit to the pond, Hannah was very excited about the frogs she had seen all around and in the pond. She described how they hid under the water with only their noses peeking out. Hannah then went to the design table and created her own frog pond.

Hannah's Description of the Frog Pond

My frog pond is in the shade to keep the frogs cool. The frogs need logs to hide under and lily pads to jump on. The water is cool to keep their skin 'fresh.'

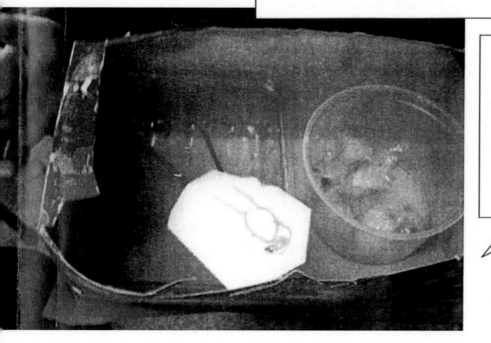

Context

Tyler started at the school in reception at the beginning of the year. He attended a pre-school for three session per week and spent the rest of the time at home with mum and younger brother Jack.

Tyler loves the outdoors and spends a lot of time exploring and investigating. He will spend quite a lot of time on his own but he willing to allow other children to join him and play alongside him. Tyler is keen to discuss and share anything interesting that he finds. He will ask questions to clarify his thinking and find out more.

Tyler's parents provide a lot of experiences for him and he often has lots to say about outings they have been on. The family often go camping but he has also experienced travelling abroad for the first time this year.

Tyler is one of the school's eco-warriors which involves working with a group of children from across the school to look after the environment, making sure people recycle and save energy.

The Headteacher talked to the school about a recent trip to Sierra Leone. A picture was shown of the waste ground next to their 'link school' which showed lots of rubbish. When asked about what the children thought Tyler commented;
"They need Eco-warriors like us to help keep it all clean and tidy."

Small group activity outside
Tyler was keen to join the group making the wormery. He handled the worms and said " It is wiggly and cold. It has lots of lines on it's body." He noted that the worms had some difference in colour saying "Some are brown and some are pinky red."

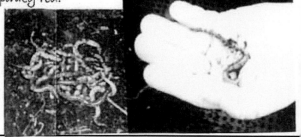

In the outdoor area Tyler found a ladybird. He showed it to Miss Metcalf. "Look at this ladybird, its got lots of spots". He counted 6 spots accurately. Tyler let the ladybird crawl on his hand. "Shall I find it a leaf to eat?" said Tyler. Billy joins them, "Here give it this." Billy gives Tyler a dandelion leaf. The ladybird opens its wings. Tyler - "Look Miss Metcalf it's trying to fly." Tyler decided to make a home for the ladybird and went to get a container to put the ladybird in.

The following week, Tyler decided to look for ladybirds again. He looked on the plant and found one. He carefully put it on his hand and looked closely at it. "I'm going to put it in the water" he said. He then put the ladybird into the water stream. "It doesn't like it...it's dying" said Tyler and he got he ladybird out of the stream.

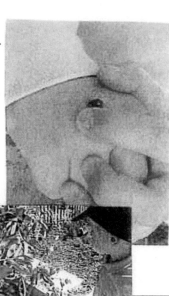

After sending a postcard from his holiday Tyler told the class all about his trip. "We stayed in a hotel. There was me and Jack, mummy, daddy and grandma. It was really hot and we had to use lots of sun cream. From our room we could see the sea and the beach. In the afternoon all the shops shut because the shop keepers have a sleep, it is called a siesta. I liked travelling on the aeroplane but it was a bit scary when we went through the clouds because the plane bumped around a lot."

Home/School Links

Things I like at home...
I like playing football with my dad and playing with my in the garden with Jack.

Things I like at school...
Playing outside, digging and going to the field. I really like Eco-club.

Things I think my child is good at...
Tyler loves to explore outside and is always asking questions about the bugs and insects he finds in the garden. He is really enjoying football now he has started going to football club on the weekend and is getting quite good. He is also really good at making sure we don't leave lights on and "save the environment" He takes being an eco-warrior very serious!

Whilst planting seeds in the vegetable garden Tyler compared the sizes of the seeds. "These seeds are very small. " He was able to identify that the carrot and the broccoli seeds were much smaller than the pumpkin seeds. When asked he was able to count our ten pumpkin seeds.

Whilst working in the group Tyler was keen to discuss his previous experiences of gardening with his grandparents;
"I planted some seeds at Grandma's once. There was lettuce and sunflower's. Grandma was really cross because the snails and slugs ate the lettuce leaves but Grandad made some netting to go over them so they couldn't do it again".

Tyler regularly visited the vegetable garden to see how the plants were growing. He was observed commenting how the plants were "big now" and looked at the different shapes of the leaves on the different plants.

Tyler works as part of a group to make pancakes on Shrove Tuesday. He is able to use the whisk effectively to beat the eggs and talks about how the colour changes as the eggs are beaten. He passes the jug to Harry to allow him to have a turn at beating the eggs. When the flour is added to the mixture Tyler comments that the mixture is "thick and gloopy". When asked what will happen to the batter in the pan Tyler replies "it will turn into a pancake and won't be all runny anymore."

Observation notes:

Puts coat on and chose to go outside.
Chooses to play with the car mat and garage.
Rolls cars down the ramp.
Negotiates with AC which cars to have.
"Let's get ones with big wheels 'cause then they'll go really fast!"

Takes cars on a journey which leads to construction area.
points to a building of the Eiffel tower on display.
"Let's build that!"
Concentrates balancing bricks to construct a tall tower.
Refers back to the picture frequently. Looks at AC's building.
"I've done this massive tower. Look how high it is."
AC says "Mine's school. Look that's where Miss parks her car".
"You can tell mine's really far away 'cause it's got a spike on top. Yours hasn't."

Context and content of observation:
OUTSIDE AREA

It is a very windy day, the girls look in the storage boxes and take out ribbons on sticks. They carefully run around avoiding other children, changing direction and laughing at the ribbons flapping about in the wind.

AR: Look they are blowing in the wind. It's very windy today. They look like flags blowing.

Context: Outdoor Area   Observer: GW
In the far corner of the mound child A and child B were working together digging a hole, looking for rabbits. The lay on their tummies and used trowels to dig the hole.
Adult: "Is that where the rabbits live then?"
Child A "Yes and they hop."
Child B "I have 1 in my garden, he visits."
Both children moved over to the bushes and began to collect leaves which they said were food for the rabbits. They moved back to the hole and pushed handfuls of leaves inside.

The Reptile Experience visit

ME was fascinated by the creatures and was
enthusiastic to hold all of them, especially the Meer Car.
She asked what the reptiles are and pulled a face saying "urgh"
when she heard the answer. She laughed as she held the
snake and described it as 'wriggly'. She said "I like all the reptiles".

DI
"We need to get the
seeds ready first and
then find some pots and
a watering can for the
water and then we will
have everything ready.
Just need soil then.

BC drew a picture
of a flower. She
looked carefully at
the size and shape
of the petals and
leaves.

Alice
"I've made a kite, I'll make sure it gets very windy. It's different from Izzy's... I'll make sure this catches the wind and hold it here and it will fly. Hold it and run!
I'm going to fly it outside, the tail will fly in the wind.
Alice and Izzy ran and held the kite up in the air but it didn't fly.
Alice – "I'm going to hang it here." (on the basket ball basket)

"Ahh yes it's flying in the wind!"

Elise
"Miss Bennett, this morning the water was frozened, but it's water now"

Why did it change?

"It got hot and it melted... it got hot with the sun"

I asked if the sun had come out, did that mean it was summer?

"No! 'Cos you can't get snow in the summer, and this was snow and iced. Maybe it's a little bit summer but most of it's winter and so it's winter, that's why."

Next, morning, Elise brought ice into school to show me it was winter.

Watching Frozen Planet (children creating their own landscapes, independent of help. They then embellished their work with objects and used the camera to take a photo)

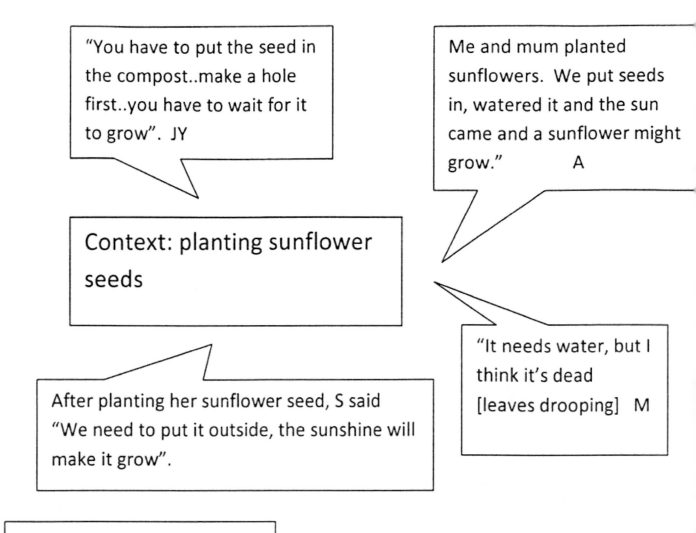

"You have to put the seed in the compost..make a hole first..you have to wait for it to grow". JY

Me and mum planted sunflowers. We put seeds in, watered it and the sun came and a sunflower might grow."   A

Context: planting sunflower seeds

After planting her sunflower seed, S said "We need to put it outside, the sunshine will make it grow".

"It needs water, but I think it's dead [leaves drooping]   M

"Mrs M the moon came out first. It's too early for the moon to come out."   J

"It's getting warmer and warmer. It's getting towards summer now. "   J

[Tasting fruit in a small group]

"smells like a special spray..you have to suck it" (lemon)

"if it's brown, it's sweet..shaped like a reindeer's claw" (banana)   K

T recognised the wheelchair sign in the school car park.

"On the way home I noticed a tree and a church".   T

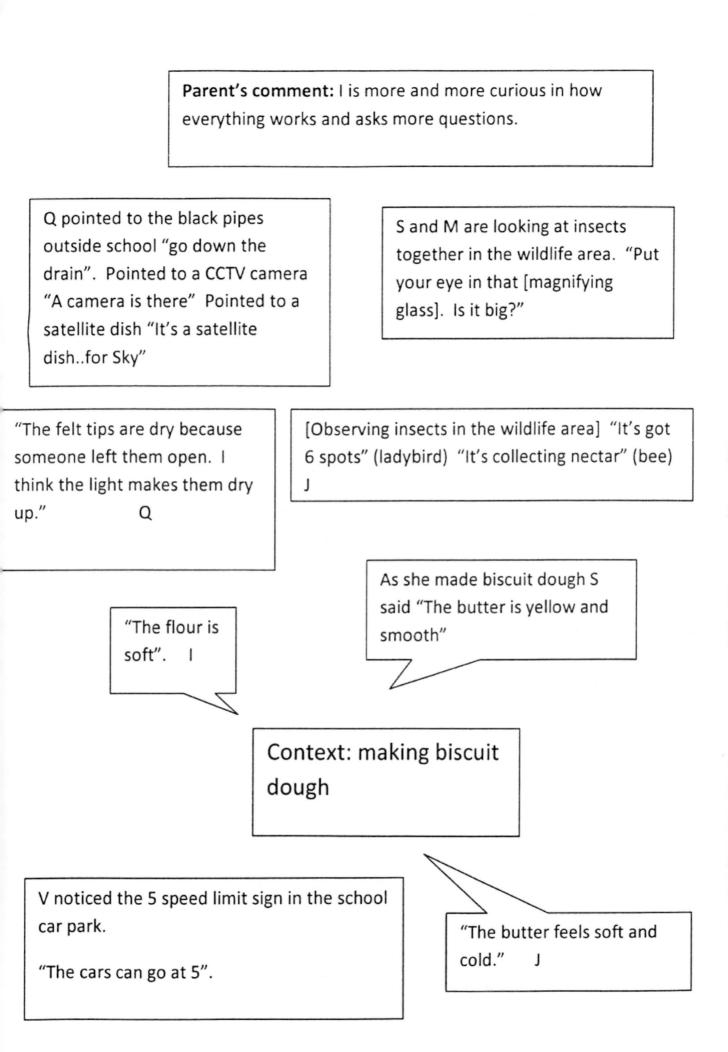

Parent's comment: I is more and more curious in how everything works and asks more questions.

Q pointed to the black pipes outside school "go down the drain". Pointed to a CCTV camera "A camera is there" Pointed to a satellite dish "It's a satellite dish..for Sky"

S and M are looking at insects together in the wildlife area. "Put your eye in that [magnifying glass]. Is it big?"

"The felt tips are dry because someone left them open. I think the light makes them dry up."   Q

[Observing insects in the wildlife area] "It's got 6 spots" (ladybird) "It's collecting nectar" (bee) J

"The flour is soft".   I

As she made biscuit dough S said "The butter is yellow and smooth"

Context: making biscuit dough

V noticed the 5 speed limit sign in the school car park.

"The cars can go at 5".

"The butter feels soft and cold."   J

EYFS Profile exemplification for the level of learning and development expected at the end of the EYFS

Understanding the world

ELG15 – Technology

Children recognise that a range of technology is used in places such as homes and schools. They select and use technology for particular purposes.

Context: J was playing in the doctor's surgery when he saw the practitioner walking past and said he needed to phone her. He pointed to the telephone on the receptionist's desk and told her that it was ringing as he dialled a number on a hands free phone.

P: Practitioner   Duration: 30-40 minutes

P: "Hello, can I help you it's the doctor's surgery."

"Ja is poorly.

P "What's the matter with him?

"He's got a poorly chin....We have to make a temperature. When I've done the temperature I'll call you back soon."

J moves over to Ja and takes his temperature with a thermometer, checks his ears with another instrument before picking up the phone again.

"He's alright now. I'll call you back now."

J presses the numbers on the hands free phone.

"I have to phone you" and he dials a number on the phone......

"I'm going to do a text to you. It's a text about poorly. It says poor-ly". *J sounds out the word as he began to text the sounds on the phone keypad.*

George made this car at home and explained how all the parts worked - even the windscreen. and headlights

(1) EF used the language, re-wind, fast forward, eject, power, loud, quiet, volume button, whilst playing in the listening area and using the CD player.

(2) EF struggles to use a pencil to form letters even when tracing over letters, however when tracing using the interactive whiteboard pens on the board he is extremely accurate.

(3) JD is able to scroll down on the computer and select an image.

(4) LF- Super mouse control on the laptop. Is able to follow instructions given by the computer and counted up to 10 objects matching them to the correct numbers on screen.

(5) MF has been helping other children on the laptops. They asked him to put "phonics play" on so MF began to type 'Phonics' into the laptop, he then looked at the drop down list and scrolled down to find the correct web address from the history. After another child saw MF do this they also asked for his help. MF can also close programmes and shut down the computers properly.

(6) When making cornflake cakes the children came to the decision that to melt the chocolate we must put it in a microwave. When we went to find the microwave one child said, "I've got one of these at home too, but I don't use it to melt things"

(7) LP shows confidence and awareness when using the computers independently. She has great mouse control and follows spoken instructions given on the computer. Also knows how to change images and created an interesting picture.

(8) FM chose to come and tell me about a power cut she had had at home. She talked about all of the things they could not do at home without electricity. "I couldn't have toast, Mummy couldn't have a cup of coffee, I couldn't watch telly and the radio didn't work."

(9) FM watched others on the computers, then felt confident to have a go at creating an image of her own using the 2simple paint programme.

Q used an old camera to 'explore' the playground. He spent a long time finding the picture he wanted to take, checking through the viewfinder many times before finally clicking the switch.

Used the touch screen paint programme at Walsall Art Gallery to draw 'his family'   Q

Q was taking photographs of his teacher. He said he had to press the red button then move the disc around

A showed good mouse control to select the correct location on 'Jump on the bus'.   Q

Selected a paint programme to use, but it was slow to start.

"It's loading"   Z

Child I went on the plasma screen and began drawing circles. She used a paint programme to mix colours. Showed good mouse control.

J drew her friend M on the plasma screen draw programme

J phones "999" in the doctor's role play

" Miss D I draw what you are wearing today"   Q

[Parent questionnaire] T has an Xbox 360 and likes to play on it at weekends.

During Health week, a WII fit board had been loaned from the Toy library. T used it independently with confidence.

"I have this game at home. I like fencing best"

child Z.

"flowers in the garden"

[Independent use of paint programme]

"I think I will see a leopard at the Safari park"

Q

Context

Georgia has been at the school throughout F1 and F2. She has a wide group of friends but a particular friendship with Lois.

She is confident in using resources throughout the unit independently and engages well in child-initiated and adult directed activity.

Georgia will talk about her ideas and often suggests ways to extend play by selecting other resources or talking about what she would like to do next. She is keen to use the camera to record her play and loves to show other children her photos and videos!

Georgia has access to a range of ICT equipment at home including a computer, a games console and karaoke machine. Her parents are keen for her to develop her use of modern technologies and allow her to use their equipment to support her learning.

Pirate Day!

As part of a whole school pirate theme day, Georgia came to school dressed up as a pirate and joined in lots of pirate activities.

Georgia made a treasure map on the computer, using the mouse effectively and selected the colours and techniques she needed.

Georgia worked in a small group to direct her beebot around the treasure map.

Parent Voice

Home/school diary entry

On Saturday Georgia and her cousin Milly used the karaoke machine to perform a concert for me and her auntie. They sang along to the songs and made up dances for each one!

Incidental discussion with parent at the beginning of the day-

"Georgia has a picture in her bag for you. She made it on her dad's computer. I was amazed at how well she can draw using the mouse. She's already much better than me on the computer....it's scary!!!"

Parental contribution to the 'Wow Board'

Georgia helped to make party invitations on the computer. She was able to type her friends names on each one.

Long observation during child-initiated activity

In the outdoor area Georgia and Lois are dancing on the stage. They each have ribbon sticks and move them to the rhythm of the music. When the track ends Lois says "Put that one on again, I like it." Georgia uses the rewind button and selects the track again. The girls both dance again. When the track finished Georgia says "Lets ask if we can make a video like Miss Tate did last week". Georgia goes inside and asks Miss Tate if we can use the video on her camera to record hers and Lois' dance. Miss Tate sets the camera to video mode and tells Georgia how to start recording. "Let's take it in turns. You video me first, then I'll do you." Georgia shows Lois how to start recoding. The girls record each others dance.

At the end of the day during story time, Georgia asked to show their video to the class.

During a letters and sounds session Georgia went with the group on a listening walk. The children walked around the school and grounds to discover all the different sounds they could hear.

Georgia was responsible for the recorder and used it to record each sound. She was able to use the start and stop buttons and with some support rewound and re-played each one to check it had recorded properly. Georgia was able to suggest moving the position of the microphone nearer to the computer keyboard when recording clicks of the office staff typing.

Georgia did ask to swap jobs with Alex and took a turn at using the camera to take a picture of door buzzer at the school entrance. She used the digital camera effectively.

On return to the classroom the children worked with Mrs Scott to upload the pictures onto the computer. The children then presented their pictures and recordings to the rest of the class.

Incidental observation   Georgia said "I'm really good at adding. Daddy let's me play an adding game on his Ipod Touch. We have a race to see who can get the most right in the time"

Mrs Goodwin the cook talked to the children about all the equipment used to cook the school lunches. She showed them the huge oven, freezer and fridges. Georgia was able to talk about why the cook uses a freezer - "Food goes in the freezer to make it really cold. When it is hard and icy the bugs and germs can't make the food go off".

asked if she could take some
photos. She handled the camera carefully
and after being shown was able to look at
the photos she had taken and show her
friends. She allowed a friend to have a turn
with the camera and showed them how to
use it, she carefully explained that
you needed to make sure your fingers
didn't cover the lens.

JG chose a CD to
play and made sure
the headphones are
plugged in. He uses
the buttons to play,
pause and rewind
the songs. He says "I
sing these songs at
home with Mummy."

HA puts 'Lamby' in
the back of the
constructa-bot. He
pushes the buttons
to make him go
forwards, backwards
and turn. He enjoys
taking Lamby for a
ride around the
classroom!

KL explored the OHP using small animals to make shadows and create a story.

With an adult in the staffroom, using the photocopier to copy his work. RI says "Can I take a copy home for my mum?" Adult nods. RI presses number 2 and the green button. He watches and then takes his work from the tray and says "Wow, this is a clever machine."

RI chooses the constructabot to use as a police car in the outdoor area. He pushes the buttons for 'forward' and 'go'. He repeats this several times as he directs the bot through his legs.

CH typed her name to log on. She then choose 'Fizzy's Number Skills' game. She could confidently follow instruction and used the mouse and keyboard to make her selections.

Children displaying high levels of involvement unscrewing old laptops leading onto language related to how things work and why.

Using 'real' tools, spanners, screw drivers and having the freedom to explore fully.

Semi is exploring the torches and coloured filters. He selects different filters and experiments with just one colour and then two. He is interested in shining the torch into the dark spaces of the planchest drawers, "I can see!"

He explores how the torch works and discovers that the light goes off if he twists the top, "it's not working."

He uses the switch to control the light, "I'm putting light in there, I'm putting light!" "It's purple," "I'm looking inside," "I can see under."

"You have to switch the button, look, on and off." He explains how to work the torch to his friend Adam. Adam says "when you're finished using it you have to switch it off because otherwise it will run out, that's what my Mum says. My batteries ran out at home."

- A child and her mum come over to the computer and the child logs on. She goes into a programme and brings up a class picture. She tells her mum the names of the people in the photo. They talk about different people in the class.

- Child selects a programme about making a sandwich. 'You click on the bread and it flies down'. Then you click on the butter, you have to wait'.

- This photo is at the beach. I'm riding a go-cart. I had to put my foot on the brake to make it stop.

- We took ages to print this out because the new printer wasn't working, it kept printing cardboard with nothing on it!

- ------ uses a camera to take a picture of her model. I look there and press this button. I can't take lots of pictures on it because it gets full. Child goes to another small group she wants to turn the camera off 'You need to push the orange button and hold it down.' said a child in the group.

William displayed his skills and knowledge of using the Bee-Bots when he chose to make up a great maths game! He was able to program the Bee-Bot accurately to move forward and backwards along the magic path to collect the objects and transport them to the correct character! 'I can make him do everything without even stopping ... watch this!' William was able to use the turn button to complete this task ... 'Forward 3, turn and forward 4,' he said 'or you could just do it easy by doing forward 3 and backwards 4!'

William drew this picture on the Interactive White Board using Active Primary. He is able to choose a new page and change the colour and size of the pen too!

EYFS Profile exemplification for the level of learning and development expected at the end of the EYFS

Expressive arts and design

ELG16 – Exploring and using media and materials

Children sing songs, make music and dance, and experiment with ways of changing them. They safely use and explore a variety of materials, tools and techniques, experimenting with colour, design, texture, form and function.

During a music session Daniel asked to use the drum with a beater. He copied the modelled example and hit the drum slowly and loudly. He then said he knew that he could make the drum make a different sound. He then beat it quickly and lightly to make a new sound.

Tyler found a short grey plastic stick in the creative area. He picked it up and held it in his hand and said to the adult that it reminded him of the microphones they had in the role play area. He then found some paper and scrunched it up to make a ball shape. He then asked an adult to help him stick the paper to the stick. He knew that glue wouldn't work and asked the adult to find some of the really sticky tape they sometimes used. He then used his microphone to sing some songs into.

Ruby and Hannah were excited by being outside on a windy day. They asked the adults to fetch the box of ribbons from the shed. They stood on the steps and pretended that it was a stage. They made up some movements using the ribbons and cheer leader pom poms. They did the same movements and in time with each other.

Observation
Ruby is on "the stage" in the classroom singing with the microphone with two other children. She starts to sing "The Wheels on the bus" and the other children play along, one with a tambourine, the other with the xylophone. She stops singing to help the two other children play along in time, and then she starts up again. Ruby sings one verse in her usual singing voice, then the next verse with a very high pitch, and a final verse in a very low pitch."

Ruby's mum says that she loves the X-Factor. She sings her favourite X-Factor songs at home.

Ruby puts some music on the CD player and dances to the rhythm of the music on the classroom stage, using a scarf as prop. She dances with the scarf wrapped round her, and then takes it off, puts it down, and picks up a silky scarf which she wafts around her as she dances.

Ruby has been observed using the following materials and tools in the creative workshop area:

- Dough: cutters and the garlic press
- Woodwork: hammer, nails, screws, screwdriver
- Painting: powder paints, ready-mix paints, bubble painting, string painting. Ruby has mixed her own colours.
- Printing: a range of natural materials
- Joining: nails, screws, PVA glue, glue stick, weaving.

Expressive arts, designing and making
Elliot was experimenting with the musical instruments. "When I bang these together they make a crash."
Elliot worked with a friend and made a transformer laser. Then they used the instruments to make some laser music.
Giacomo showed TA how to use lots of instruments to make different noises. "You hit the different notes. You have to hit slowly and gently to make it quiet."

Saskia chose the colours she wanted to create her painting. She selected black paper from the paper available and used 2 brushes at the same time. She said it was like the 'spikey dance' we did in the hall!

Chloe and Izzy are at the music table. I is using a wood block as a microphone and the other is using the castanets to tap in time to the song. I and D join in and they organise themselves. D asks "What can I use", he selects a triangle. They sing together and use the instruments carefully – using the songs they have learned for their phonics. D sings "Twinkle, twinkle chocolate bar" after they have chosen bells to go with the song. Desmond makes up lyrics with the girls' names, which makes them all laugh.

D selects the spoons and explores the different sounds they make.

Keira has worked with her sister and a Year 2 boy to make this octopus and grass. Keira was given the job of sellotaping each blade of grass to the picture! She can use the sellotape dispenser with great success! She cut the paper to make the horizontal joins for each individual piece.

Zoe

Working in the creative area she is selecting resources and spends time feeling them and experimenting on how to fix them to a piece of paper. She uses a glue stick to enable her to fix wood shavings onto the paper.

She selects black paper and a white chalk and draws her mum with careful strokes.

She sees another child has made a fan and carefully folds a piece of paper to make her own. She selects tape and scissors from the resource area and carefully cuts a small piece of tape which she folds around the end to secure it. She is pleased with the result. "My fan". She then selects some blue paper and cuts a small shape which she matches carefully to the 'handle'. She matches the cut paper to the side to check it fits. She chooses different colours and cuts shapes which she adapts until she is happy with them.

She explains that "this bit sticks it" and demonstrates how she uses the green shape to hold the fan shut.

During the 'dads to school day' L. E. and their dad investigated whether they could make different shaped bubbles.

Context

During child initiated activities Thomas regularly spends time in the workshop area of the classroom. He can confidently use scissors, glue sticks, paintbrushes and rollers and can use a wide variety of joining materials for a specific purpose. Throughout the year his creations have become more imaginative and he enjoys experimenting with different materials and textures to give a desired effect.

Thomas knows a variety of nursery rhymes and simple songs and always joins in when the whole class is singing. During child initiated activities Thomas can often be observed singing to himself. He is able to adapt songs and change the words within his songs, often to the amusement of others!

Throughout the year Thomas has enjoyed exploring the different sounds instruments can make, especially when playing with his peers. Thomas understands language such as loud, quiet, fast and slow and is able to use this when playing with the instruments.

Observation

After a class input on Dawili Thomas made a Diva lamp. He confidently modelled the clay into a pot shape using his fingers. He then took a paint brush and used the pointed end to make circle shapes on the sides of his lamp.

Observation

Thomas spent a long time creating this tool belt. He could describe the function of each piece. He used different techniques, treading, rolling, gluing and sellotaping the pieces together. He collected all the resources he needed by himself and worked with concentration and perseverance until the task was complete. He was very proud of his achievement.

Observation

Whilst painting Thomas was able to mix his own paints knowing that yellow and red made orange and that blue and red made purple.

Observation

Thomas was using the wooden spoons out of the music making box. He explored the different sounds the spoons make as he hit different surfaces around the playground. He then found the pans and trays and made his own music station.

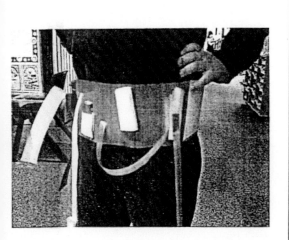

Home School Links

Name: Thomas

What am I good at when I am at School
* I like playing in the workshop area, using the scissors, glue sticks, split pins, paperclips, pencils and boxes to make pictures and models.
* I like singing at group time with Mrs Davis.

What am I good at when I am at home
* At home I like playing with my work bench. Dad helps me to cut the wood with the saw and hammer the nails. I like it when mum lets me paint my models.

Three things my parents say I am good at…
* Using tools… scissors, hammer, saw, vice, different sized paint brushes.
* Sing and dancing with his sister when playing on Just Dance on the Wii.
* Singing songs with his mummy and changing the words

Something me and my family think I would really like to learn more about at school…
• painting and mixing colours

Observation

Whilst playing with train track Thomas sang to himself …" They're two, they're four, they're six, they're eight, shunting trucks and hauling freight red and green and brown and blue they're the really useful crew…." Thomas was confident with the song and repeated it several times whilst joining the train tracks together and moving the trains on the railway line.

Name:	Date:
A G R	

Observation and context:
In the Cinderella role play area, and all were dressed up. A was pretending to be Cinderella and was sweeping the floor with the brush.
G was pretending to be a step sister. "Do my dinner!" G demanded. "Please can I go to the ball?" A pleaded. "No you can't." G answered. "Turn Cinderella into a nice dress" R said as she pretended to wave a wand at A.
"Pass some more food!" G said. "No you have to eat what I have given you" replied A.

Child initiated

Name:	Date:
A	

Observation and context:
In the workshop making a model of a phone.
"I've put the batteries in there" A said as he stuck an extra part on.

Child/~~adult~~ initiated
"Look at my phone" A said as he put it to his ear. "Look at the batteries" he continued.
A talked through his actions as he worked.

A spent 15 mins working in the workshop. He was proud of his model, and explained, "it's an electric phone I put the batteries in (indicating a space). "That's the pen, I can press the buttons with it."
A had used masking tape to fix the pieces together and drawn a grid for the front of the phone. There was a 'pen' attached with a ribbon to the phone.

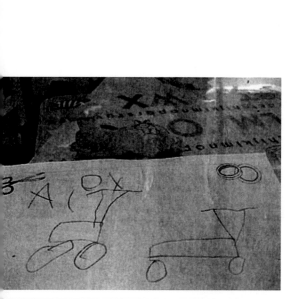

Name: A	Date:

Observation and context:
"I'm going to design a scooter."
A drew 2 scooters.
"I've made a big design and a little design."
"I've got a great idea how to make the wheels." He rolled some playdough in his hands to make a ball. A went on to make a scooter with 2 wheels, handlebars and a platform.
"It needs 3 wheels because that bit is flat on the ground" he said as he added a wheel to support the platform.
"Now I've designed a skateboard as well."

Child/adult initiated

<u>Parent page</u>

A has really settled down this term. He is sleeping better and I think this has helped him concentrate more at school.

For Xmas he got a big box of lego for children aged 5+. He has surprised us with the complicated structures he has constructed.

He often talks about numbers and likes to play around with adding and subtracting imagined or real objects.

He loves to sing and make up his own rhymes. A's imaginary play has blossomed; he can construct entertaining scenarios using soft toys or toy cars/construction toys. He has made lots of friends this term and talks fondly of Z L and M.

We really value comments about your child's learning both at school and at home and are grateful for your contributions.
Many thanks.

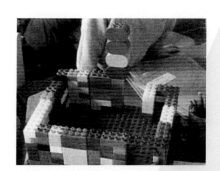

A 'Wow' star from home

A is making some amazing models at home. He is inventing things that have a purpose, like, special containers for his craft materials. He is also learning to put away his craft materials in his own special cupboard.

Name: A	Date:

Observation and context:
A really enjoyed the clay work this afternoon. She was completely absorbed and smiled for much of the time. She worked with the clay for at least 20 mins smoothing the surface which she wet repeatedly. She was happy to share a lump with Toby and enjoyed, squashing and squeezing the clay into different shapes enjoying the tactile experience.

Child initiated activity

A chose to work at the computer. She drew a butterfly using 'Primary Paint'. Well done! You have tried really hard to make both sides the same!!

Parent page

A has settled really well at school. She comes home singing new songs and talking about new friends. She is enjoying all the play, arts and fun of the class R. Thank you for settling her so well!

A often chooses to work in the malleable area and loves the playdough. She can competently roll out dough, use cutters efficiently and a variety of tools on hand, eg. sticks, extruders etc. Here she has used her fingers to press out the butterfly wings. Then rolled the blue playdough to form 6 legs. "Those are the legs, those are the antennae and that's the tail", she said pointing to each part.

A will often choose to paint and regularly uses both the ready mixed paint on the easel, or the colour mixing table. She selected her paper and mixed the colours she wanted in the palette. When she had finished she took her brush and palette to the sink and washed them up competently before putting them out again for the next child to use.

A beautiful symmetrical ladybird.

A played "That loud?" ch -
'Yes that's how loud I want
t. Just that pink one pointing
:o the xylophone". She
:hen accompanied A on the
wooden block.
A played along the scale
iitting each note and then
oulled the beater along all
:he notes and then repeated.
They were happy for other
children to then come and
oin them.

Child initiated

A chose to work in the mark making area and was absorbed
in colouring and patterned squares on her Elmer for at least
20 mins. She could describe the different patterns she had
used. Having patterned about half the squares she then
coloured in the remainder.

Making stripes for the wasps. Carefully
olling tiny pieces of playdough

Name: A	Date:

Observation and context:
A really enjoys our singing lessons and is becoming increasingly
confident to join in. This afternoon she was happy to be one of
a small group of children performing the actions in front of the
key stage. She knew all the words and used the whole range of
accompanying actions. Later in the day she was singing all of the
songs with a group of friends in the classroom at the playdough table.

Adult directed

An Autumn pattern
I've made a buzzy bee. Look it's got a shell
ead and those cute wings."

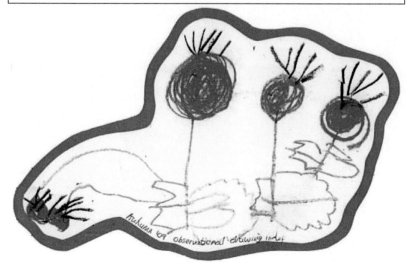

I watched from afar. This was about 40 mins of exploration and investigation

Outdoor area exploration and investigation of resources and natural materials.

40 minutes concentration and application.

Children making swirling patterns
using 'white paint'. The children wanted
to add glitter and snowflakes to make
it like 'frosty' from the story.

Some children were exploring the digging
area and Grace's mentioned it squelched
like the mud from 'The Bear hunt'. The
class teacher encouraged making 'mud' and
the children investigated how to do this.
I'm stuck Mrs. Clarke, said Grace, the mud
has glued my wellies!

The children explored feeling the mud with
their feet and with their hands. They made
hand prints on the fence and scrap paper
on the floor! This investigation was on
the back of exploring the book 'The Bear hunt'.

Poppy's music – A learning story

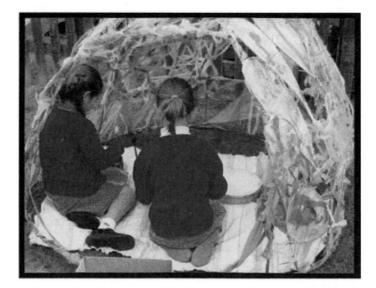

Poppy and Julia chose to play the chime bars together. When Poppy became aware that I was listening, she said; "it sounds like the bells at church". I told Poppy that the bells called people to church on a Sunday morning and Poppy replied; "that's what happened in Cinderella. The church bells woke her up". Poppy played both the F and G# chime bars, hitting both of them gently to make a tune. I got some more chime bars out of the box for Poppy and she hit them gently in turn to make a tune. She seemed pleased with the tune she was making. Poppy told me how her brother Harry makes tunes; "not with instruments but with his mouth". She later said; "that one (C#) sounds like the end of a song!" – it was the last chime bar in her row. Julia listened to the tune that Poppy was playing and said; "that makes a nice song".

Poppy asked Julia; "do you want to make my tune bigger?" They added more chime bars to the row and played together, making the tune longer. Poppy said; "if we practice more we'll be really good at instruments".

Poppy continued to play the chime bars by herself and made spontaneous comments such as; "that's not a very nice sound" (when she accidently put her finger on the chime bar as she hit it with the beater) and; "I've found an 'E' one!" She asked me to; "come and look at this!" and played me a tune of quick notes that went across all of the assembled chime bars.

Cameron joined Poppy and initially played the tambour with the beaters. He then joined Poppy in playing the chime bars. When Cameron played the chime bars loudly, Poppy said; "You have to do a quiet tune!" Cameron replied; "I'll do a really loud one!" and hit the chime bars hard. As Cameron played the chime bars, Poppy began to play the tambourine with a beater, saying; "I've added the tambourine to it [Cameron's tune]".

Later, Poppy played maracas whilst Cameron played the chime bars and a maraca. When Cameron left, Poppy played both maracas (one in each hand) and shook them gently, swaying from side to side as she played. Poppy said; "I'm really good at instruments!" She then played a maraca and the tambourine together, keeping a steady beat as she played them. She was keen to see how many instruments she could play at one time and said; "I'm going to play three… then four!" Poppy shook the bells and the tambourine with one hand and used the maraca as a beater on the skin of the tambourine with the other hand. As she did so she said; "the drumming helps the maraca bits to move".

At 10:15 Poppy said; "I'm really tired!" and stopped playing with the instruments. She had been playing for nearly one hour!

Julia chose to make a clay butterfly and spent an afternoon making it. She was keen to paint it and once it was dry painted the front and sides very carefully, checking that she had not left any parts of her model unpainted (child initiated).

Ella chose to use the marker pens and filled a piece of A3 paper with patches of colour

Julia created a rainbow with the chalks on the Reception playground. Child initiated

Will made up his own song to the tune of 'I Hear Thunder'.

"Father Christmas, Father Christmas;

With the toys, with the toys;

For me and all the children, for me and all the children;

Yes he did, yes he did".

Harriet, Euan, Jaden, Louis, Poppy and Thomas took the toy snake for a walk. Harriet held the head and as they walked around the classroom she said; "who wants to ride Mr Snake? The children also sang; "I like to ride Mr Snake... it's not very far". Harriet also made up another song for the snake; "say 'goodbye' to the pictures, say 'hello' to the Lego, say 'hello' to the pictures" as they moved around (child initiated).

After a heavy rainfall at lunchtime, children were inspired by their puddle splashing to represent raindrops.

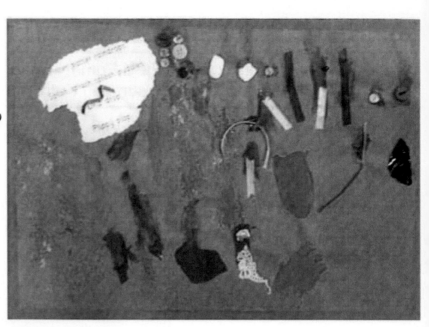

At the weekend, S went to a bonfire celebration.

On Monday, she confidently accesses a range of materials exploring the texture and colour of each. S investigated the properties of materials by layering, scrunching, twisting and folding them.

A spent a long time experimenting with the contrasting textures found in the variety of natural materials.

'I love the smooth shiny conkers' she told the practitioner.

J   looked very closely at the leaves outside and used 'Fresco' (art software) to re-create his experience

"this is soft like the petals."

child's voice

He selected resources from 'junk' to make skis. He realised that the skis needed to be attached to his feet, so he punched holes in the top, so he could place his feet inside the boxes to move the skis

Hannah uses a variety of materials, tools and techniques to construct a beautiful butterfly.
She goes on to paint, use oil pastels, chalk pastels and inks to create more butterflies.
She explores the patterning of symmetry and the properties of paper to make her butterflies fly in the garden.
Hannah and her friends make up their own songs, make music and dance as they explore the notion of the beautiful butterfly.
Hannah, Aleah and Molly use existing stories and songs as a framework and experiment with ways of changing them.

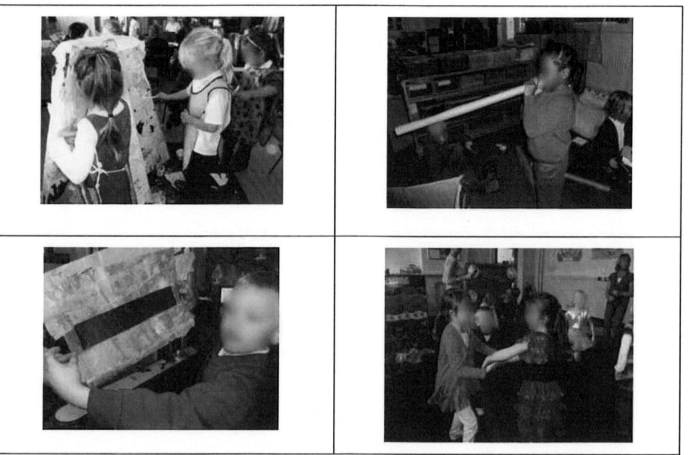

To make a snowman for a whole school Christmas display a group of children cover several large boxes with white paint. One of them comments that the paint doesn't stay on the box very well. They decide that they need to cover it with something else as well. Between them they request that the adult goes to the art cupboard to find the ' lovely smooth, silky, sparkly material' that they had seen before during a session on wedding celebrations. They also requested some cotton wool and some tissue paper.

Sosan used a long cylinder that has been discarded from the junk modelling area and begins to experiment making sounds down the tube. She is delighted with what she hears and then begins to hum a song that the children have been learning in class.

After watching a session on the IWB about the Northern lights Ben went to the creative area and found some coloured tissue paper. He then proceeded to tear it in to long strips because the images had been long and thin. He selected a light green colour and then commented that he liked the way it changed colour when it was stuck on to the blue paper. Lastly he added a purple strip as there had been a very vivid purple image on the screen

Poppy and Hannah link hands during a session where a surprise party has been given to an adult. They make up a short dance by moving around in a circle one way and then back again. They finish their routine by stopping and holding their hands together up high.

EYFS Profile exemplification for the level of learning and development expected at the end of the EYFS

Expressive arts and design

ELG17 – Being imaginative

> **Children use what they have learnt about media and materials in original ways, thinking about uses and purposes.**
> **They represent their own ideas, thoughts and feelings through design and technology, art, music, dance, role play and stories.**

Context:

Georgia is able to demonstrate her imaginative skills through her modelling and role play. She enjoys sharing stories with both adults and peers and she is able to recreate / develop roles throughout the environment, for example, in the home corner, on the stage and when playing with the puppet theatre.

Georgia is often observed in the outdoor environment practising her dance moves and enjoys teaching the others what she has learnt at dance class the previous week! She is clearly developing a specific taste in music as when dancing she seems to prefer music which has a faster beat.

During child initiated activities Georgia can often be found exploring and experimenting with the paints, glue and fabrics. She enjoys creating her own collages and is happy to talk about her work with both peers and adults within the class.

Recently Georgia has shown a growing interest in recording her work and that of her peers through the use of the digital camera. Georgia is able to use the digital camera confidently to take pictures. Georgia is able to identify the image she would like to take and, with the aid of the adult, she can download her work and share it with the rest of the group on the interactive white board.

Observation:

Georgia asked Mrs Kay if she could use the digital camera. Georgia confidently took a picture of her model and showed the image back to the teacher. Mrs Kay helped Georgia download the image so that it could be shared with the class on the interactive whiteboard. Georgia confidently discussed her work with the class.

Observation:

Georgia mixed the powder paints independently knowing the sequence "water, sponge and paint mix."

Observation:

Whilst in the home corner Georgia selected the different fruits she would like to take to her friend Charlotte. Whilst she did this she was able to tell Yasmin why Charlotte would like the tangy purple passion fruit.

Context:

During focused group activities Georgia has been talking about seasons and change. She has enjoyed talking about the changes in weather and how this impacts on her everyday life. She has been particularly interested in the changes of colour.

Observation:

After collecting twigs and bark from outside with Florrie, Georgia took the powder paints and began to mix the yellow, blue and red together. Once she had achieved the correct shade of brown, and it was of the right consistency, Georgia painted the bark, stating "this is tricky as the bark is all bumpy." Georgia persevered and then moved onto painting the twig. Once complete Georgia used the bark and twigs in her autumn picture collage.

Observation:

Whilst outside playing with the scarves Georgia selects a pop CD and places it in the CD player. Charlotte says "put on track 12, that's my favourite." Georgia finds the song and says "yeah I like this song, it's fast." Together they dance with the scarves in time to the music. As the song finishes a slower song starts. Georgia stops dancing and says "this song is too slow, lets do the other song again?" The girls repeated the dance for song 12.

Home School Links

Name: *Georgia*

What do I enjoy when I am at School

* *I like dancing to the pop music outside on the stage.*

* *I like taking pictures with Mrs Frary on the digital camera. I like to talk about them on the interactive white board.*

What do I enjoy when I am at home

* *I like playing with my puppet theatre. My sister likes to play with me.*

* *I like helping daddy when he is taking pictures with his camera.*

Three things my parents say I am good at…

* *Playing with her older sister when telling stories using the puppet theatre.*

* *Dancing.*

* *"Drawing, cutting and sticking" using things from the "making box."*

Something me and my family think I would really like to learn more about at school…

* *Continue to develop Georgia's interest in stories and how she uses this in all aspects of her work.*

Home / School Links:

Achievement: Georgia achieved her Grade 1 dance award this weekend. Mummy and Daddy are proud of her.

During free flow time Kelise was at a table cutting out spiral shapes that had been pre-drawn for firework pictures. She stood at the table and cut out her spiral, when finished she put it up to her head and said it looked like hair. She then went and found some paper and made a headband and stuck the spiral on to the band and declared that she was now Rapunzel. She then repeated the action twice more until she had three long strands of paper hanging from her headband. She then went outside and climbed up into the small house at the top of the slide and put her head out ensuring that the long paper hair strands were hanging down. 'Now I'm Rapunzel in her castle'.

During free flow time Isabelle visited the creative are and found a card that had been discarded from a game. Isabelle picked it up and held it up, she folded it around to join the edges and said it looked like a lantern that her family had in the garden during the summer. She found the glue and stuck it together. She then said she need some 'soft yellow paper' to make it look like a light. She self selected some yellow tissue paper and stuck it onto the inside of her lantern. She was extremely proud of her achievement and proudly took it home at the end of the day and told the adult that she had 'designed' a lantern.

Beth selected a programme on 2Simple. She explored a variety of tools and exclaimed, 'fireworks without the bang!' She selected different colours and sizes to create an explosion of colour just like the fireworks she saw on the telly.

When the painting was finished they realised that it was too wet to use as a rocket.

Emily declared that it needed drying off. She reached for some paper and started fanning it quickly, other children came and joined in. 'It's still too wet!'

She turned to the adult and asked her if she had a hair dryer in school. The adult replied that she hadn't but she did know where there was a dryer in school. Emily jumped up and took the box into the cloakroom and placed it under the hand drier. She was thrilled when the paint was dry and the children spent some considerable time role-playing in the box and going off to the moon.

Zain comes into reception with his dad. He is carrying a shield which he had made at home using paper, sellotape and felt-tips. He tells the teacher, "it's a shield to fight the baddies." Zain's dad says that he is always having to bring scrap paper home from the office for Zain to make things with. He is always making props at home to go with his superhero play.
The next day, Zain makes a cape out of paper. He says, "I've made a cape. If you press this sellotape button and then the fighting things come out of my cape when I say it. When I take it off I load this point and it turns into a sword."

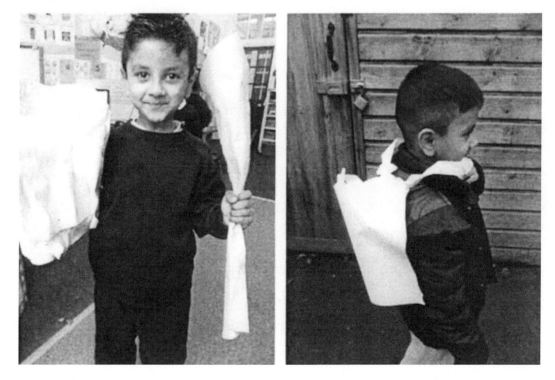

During time when the group were working on the story of the Three Little Pigs a group of boys declared that they wanted to be builders. They discussed that they wanted to make strong houses made from bricks. They organised themselves to go outside and requested the builders role play box. They used the equipment and put on hats and then proceeded to act out building a wall, using a trowel to put on the cement and to smooth it down.

Maddison takes on the role of the foreman when she is working in the role play construction site. She tells Joe that during the night part of the building had collapsed and that the job he had to do today was to make the area safe. She told him that she had already put up the danger sign to warn others not to come too close.

Hannah found some paper that had a brick pattern printed on it. She then found a large box and declared that she was going to make a model of her bedroom. She carefully covered the inside of her box with the paper. When she had finished with the box she used the small world furniture to furnish the room with appropriate furniture.

Charlie listed the things that he would put in his knapsack when he was acting out the part of the third little pig. He commented that he would need some clothes to wear, some food to eat and that he would need to take a toothbrush so that he could clean his teeth.

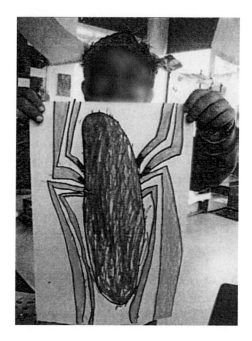

Hiresh spent sustained time using blocks to make a spacecraft – showed knowledge of main features of symmetry, wings, and cockpit.

Hiresh worked away quietly on the craft table, eventually emerging with a blue spider – completely independent work!

Hiresh collected leaves and berries from the bushes for friends to support their role playing (making 'soup').

Hiresh spent a long time making a bridge from our outdoor wooden blocks. Hiresh was very proud of his creation and insisted on a photo when finished.

Hiresh watched friends rolling tyres, and became very excited when he realised that he was able to roll a tyre too!

Hiresh joined in with friends playing bat and ball, good range of skills evident.

A wanted to make a band. He got the music box out and called some friends over.

"Which instrument do you want to use?"

Instruments were chosen and swapped around for the best sound!

"Oh listen, this one is better than the castanets."

The boys used the instruments and, after trying a few, they agreed on a short tune!

A thought it would be a good idea to make up a dance to go with their music.

"I think we should do a dance as well."

A got his friends to take turns to come to the front and do their own dance.

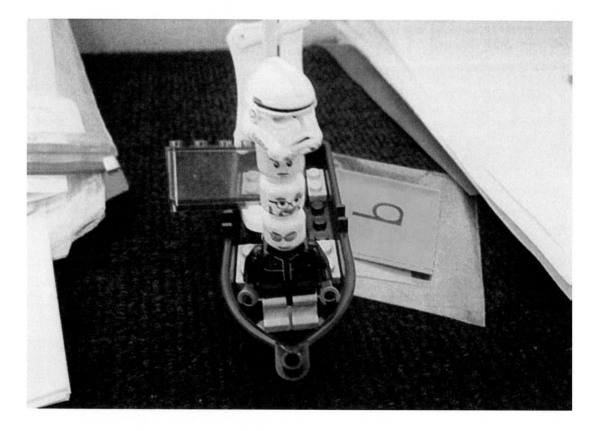

"I've made a storm trooper boat."

Oscar then placed the model on the steps.

"It's a new storm trooper for the new Star Wars film. They are making a new film, I've seen the advert on my tele at home. I think there will be a boat in the new film because there are space ships and ships are boats."

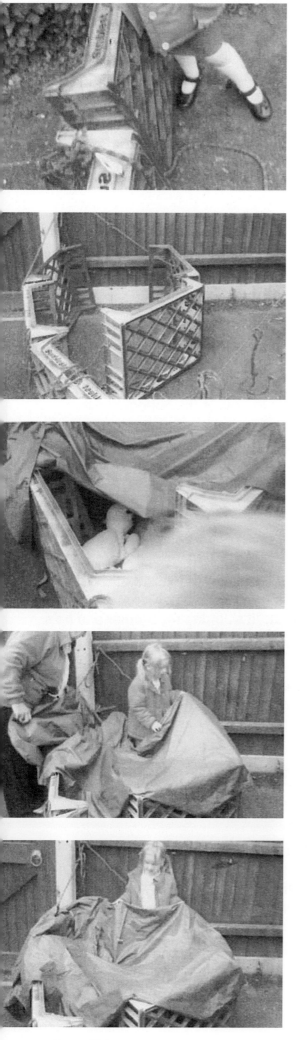

Outside area –

PW started making a wall across the corner of the playground by standing bread baskets on end. Kiera suggested they should be fixed together so they didn't fall down. Said it could be a sheep pen.

"They need a bedroom too."

Positioned more baskets to create a separate area. Found fabric to put on the floor and an old coat which she asked for help in draping over the top, 'so the rain doesn't come in'.

"We need a door so people can go in and out."

Collected a toy sheep and dog to put in the 'bedroom'. Made tickets with a 1, which she wrote on as the admission was £1! Also wrote a reminder note to Mrs Francis to bring her sheep crook and pictures of her dogs.

Cameron drew a monster on a whiteboard in the outdoor classroom alongside Corey (child initiated). I asked if the lines he was drawing were the monster's hair and he laughed and said; "No! His feet!" He made a roaring sound when he had finished his monster and then rubbed it off his board saying; "I rubbed it away!"

Cameron then began to draw a second monster on his whiteboard and said; "This one's going to look really funny… lots of teeth. He's eating a burger [as Corey's monster was too]. I'm going to do lots of teeth and then he's eating a burger." Cameron made each tooth by drawing a line from the top to the bottom of the monster's mouth.

Kieron and Edward drew alongside each other at the art table (child initiated). Kieron spoke as he drew saying; "It's Jordan my brother and he's wearing a costume – he's the Hulk… This is me and my body's going to be red".

Kieron got some paper and began to draw. As he drew he said; "I'm drawing a baddie and he's called 'Magold' 'cause he's gold." Kieron continued to draw and colour and then said (in a different voice); "What are you doing on my planet? I'm too powerful." To me he said; "He said he's too powerful, but he's not." Kieron carried on drawing and said; "One, two, three, four, next fingers. He's got one eye. Actually, I'll count them again – five fingers." Kieron began to draw a new character and talked to himself as he did so; "Green, green, yeah, green. That's one of his eyes there, smiley mouth and a nose there and a bit of a body – green." Kieron drew for over ten minutes, talking about his drawing as he did so. Child initiated.

Edward and Thomas played in the 'vets' together (child initiated). The following
formed part of their conversation as they played (J.B.);
Thomas; "Hello, my pet's [a tortoise] got hurt again".
Edward; "What's your name?"
Thomas; "Thomas Taylor".
Edward; "What does it start with?"
Thomas; "'T' [sound]". Edward types on the computer.
Edward; "Come back later today at six o'clock".
Thomas; "Thanks... He's hurt on his nose".
Edward; "I know what to do. I've got a plaster". Edward mimes putting a plaster on the
tortoise's nose.
Edward; "Bye!"
Thomas; "Bye!"

Gracie and Poppy were playing 'Princesses' outside (child initiated). Poppy said;
"Watch out! You're going to fall in the deep blue sea!" and "When the sun sets you will be
asleep for ever!" Gracie said; "Let's pretend this is the castle." Later Poppy told me that
they were playing "Sleeping Beauty" and that she was the "evil witch." Gracie was
Sleeping Beauty and Poppy told her; "now the Prince is going to kiss you Sleeping
Beauty." Corey joined the game and said; "wake up Sleeping Beauty!"

Cameron and Jaden played with the builders tools (child initiated). The following
formed part of their conversation as they played;
Cameron; "We're building a shelf."
Cameron; "I need some nails."
Jaden; "I'll do this bit."
Cameron; "Will everything fit in here?"
Cameron; "I need the drill."
Jaden; "I've got two screwdrivers."
Cameron; "I want that nail."
Cameron; "You might need one of these, Jaden."
Jaden; "It's finished!"
Cameron; "O.K."

Taylor brought me a picture she had drawn and asked me to "spot the difference".
I had to say what things were different about the flowers. I found several differences
and Taylor added some more; "it hasn't got leaves" and "the petals are bigger"

I chose to work in the Chinese takeaway. She dressed up then went to the desk.

"Noodles please."

"You have to pay. It is pretend money."

She then went to wait for her order. She stayed in role in the restaurant, 'eating' with chopsticks. Sometimes asking for more food from the waiter, sometimes returning to the desk to place an order.

I was in the reading corner with P holding one of the hand puppets. She held the puppet carefully and sang 'Rock-a-bye baby' beautifully.

"Here's his pillow" I said as she laid the lamb on the pillow.

"This needs to be wrapped around him" P said.

"Night, night, I'll stay here" said I as she got a book.

I then said "Mummy".

"I'll stay here" P said. I then pretended to try and sit on P's knee.

"Stay there" P said in a gentle voice. I asked I what she was pretending to be, and she said a cat.

Sally and I were working with a group of children in the movement play area.

S: 'we're sailing away."

I: "This is the area where I can dance." She said as she twirled around completely engaged in dancing.

S: "But we need to sail away." I got back on the boat.

S: "get back on board."

S: "waves, waves, waves" she said as she used the oar to lift scarves in the air in time to the music.

I then jumped out of the boat again and began dancing energetically with Ruby as the music had become faster.

S: "We're sailing back. Hey, you'll get stuck in the water."

Sally and I continued in these roles for a whole class session, taking turns at different roles and involving other children.

N: "please can we be dragons and make music?"

I then asked Ruby to join her and, as their play began, Leyla and Gracie joined.

I: "some of us need to make music and some of us need to dance. Let's take turns and work as a team."

The girls then took turns, alternating between music-making and dancing. They kept a steady rhythm with the instruments and, when dancing, bobbed up and down in time to the music.

They used a range of instruments selected from the music box. Their play was sustained.

Their work was in response to work done several weeks earlier, on the Chinese new year.

"5 little butterflies went flying one day over the clouds and far away..."

Hannah makes up her own story using 'The hungry caterpillar' as a reference. She uses play food to represent the foods in the original story then uses the framework to include her own favourite foods. She acts out her new story to a group of children in the class.

Hannah makes a 'beautiful butterfly' using a variety of materials and uses glue and scissors effectively.

She composes a butterfly song and dance making her own music and directing others.

Hannah represents her own ideas, thoughts and feelings through design and technology, art, music, dance, role play and stories.

"There was once a cocoon lying on top of a beautiful butterfly...

I know, we can have tinkly sounds for the butterfly's wings.

I saw a butterfly she was so beautiful in the light of the moon."

"Mrs Higgins – This is my mermaid Christmas picture. The mermaid has put up her Christmas decorations under the sea."

A has been living in Vienna and has been in England for nine months. He speaks German and Greek. He is rapidly learning English.

A is a very creative little boy and loves to create things.

A made a model of the Millennium bridge out of plasticine.

"This is the bridge on the river, it can go up like this and it can go down. It will let the boats come in"

I asked A if he had made the Millennium bridge

"yes that is right, it is near here"

Another day A came out to show me Pinocchio.

"Look I have made Pinocchio. His nose gets big"

A made a mask for Halloween.

"It is a monster, grrr. Do you like it?"

EYFS Profile exemplification
Learning journey

Communication and language

ELG01 – Listening and attention

Children listen attentively in a range of situations. They listen to stories, accurately anticipating key events and respond to what they hear with relevant comments, questions or actions. They give their attention to what others say and respond appropriately, while engaged in another activity.

Explanatory notes

The child listens actively while engaged in a variety of activities from which he or she is able to recall significant details. This includes stories and rhymes. When listening to suggestions or explanations, the child responds appropriately through actions or comments, predicting what might happen or by asking relevant questions. The child remains focused on an activity, can sustain a conversation with someone as they play and perseveres despite distractions showing consistently high levels of involvement.

November

Over the weekend, all of the leaves had fallen from one of the trees. The children were helping me to sweep and collect the leaves into bin bags. M was helping to hold open a bag, and was watching other children sweeping. J said "look, M, we've made a shape with the bag!" M turned to look at the bag and said "Oh yes! We've made a triangle! That's funny!'"

December

Outside – child initiated

During the morning session, the class had read "Peace at Last" during an adult led shared reading session. M was with two other children outside. They laid the pieces from the balancing beam out to create a large rectangular shape. M said "I'm making a house...oh no! I can't stand this! We need to make a garden now..." She collected more pieces of the balancing beam and laid these out too. She collected two chairs and placed them inside the first rectangular shape. She said "this is my bed" and lay across the seats and closed her eyes.

December

Workshop – child initiated

M held up a model she had made and said, "I've made Baby Bear a rocket! When the glue's dry I will turn it upside down and these will be where the fire comes out!"

Earlier in the week, the class had read and re-told "Whatever Next!" during adult led activities.

September

Interactive whiteboard

During free-flow session time, M was drawing and mark making on the interactive whiteboard. E came and sat on a chair next to the whiteboard. E said "what are you doing?" M continued mark making and said "look, this makes a shape...a rectangle like a doorway...and I can make a big square...look like this!" E asked, "Can I have a go?" M said "hmm, Ok." M cleaned the board with the rubber and E began to mark make. M fetched a sand timer and said, "When this runs out it's my turn again!"

M had selected black paper and chalks. She was mark making with orange chalk. As she was drawing, an adult asked, "can you tell me about what you are doing?" M continued to mark make and said "This is my firework picture...I went to my Nanni and Grandad's house. My Mummy and Daddy and J came too. We had some fireworks and a bonfire."

Role play

Following children's interests, the role-play area had been set up as a doctor's surgery. During an earlier adult led session, a book about doctors had been read to the children, and children had given ideas as to why they might go to visit a doctor, what they might see or do at a doctor's surgery. During this session, M had listened carefully as the book was read, and had given lots of ideas about doctors, from her own experiences. Later in the day she chose to play with two other children in the role play.

M said "I've got a poorly leg, but it's only a little bump!". H wrapped M's leg up with a bandage, and J checked her heart with a stethoscope!

LISTENING AND ATTENTION

Children listen attentively in a range of situations. They listen to stories, accurately anticipating key events and respond to what they hear with relevant comments, questions or actions. They can give their attention to what others say and respond appropriately while engaged in another activity.

February

During shared reading of "We're Going on a Bear Hunt", as the adult read "there's a cave...we can't go over it, we can't go under it, we'll have to go through it..." M put her hand up and said "there will be a bear in there!"

June

M was sitting in the book corner with J, looking at a book. A child from the next door class came into the book corner, pointed to the light switch and said "why is there a light switch there?". M looked up from the book, looked at where the child was pointing and said, "Because it's very dark inside the cupboard!"

February

Writing area

Earlier in the week, "We're Going on a Bear Hunt" had been read and re-told during adult led activities. "Story map" frames had also been introduced and used during previous adult led teaching. Blank frames had been left in the writing area for children to use. M picked up a story map frame and said, "I'm going to make a story map. I need grass first..." She drew, and then said, "grass, g-r-a-ss" as she wrote "grass along the first arrow. She continued drawing and talking to herself, until she had drawn pictures in each of the four boxes. M: "hmmm, water...I'm making water all around...hmmm, the snowstorm... I did the snowstorm...now I need a bear cave!".

See attachment – M's Bear Hunt Story Map

April

Outside

The Gingerbread Man had been read to children during story time the previous day.

M ran around the area, calling "Run, run as fast as you can, you can't catch me, I'm the gingerbread man!"

EYFS Profile exemplification Learning journey

Communication and language

ELG02 – Understanding

> **Children follow instructions involving several ideas or actions. They answer 'how' and 'why' questions about their experiences and in response to stories or events.**

Explanatory notes

The child is able to understand and respond to a series of simple steps in order to complete a familiar or unfamiliar activity. The child is able to answer questions about their own activities or experiences and is able to demonstrate understanding by answering questions including 'how' and 'why' about stories and events.

November

Outside adult led activity (role playing a bonfire party and keeping safe).

I asked, "what else do we need?"

M said, "we need a bucket to put the sparklers in." I said, "Please will you go inside and ask a grownup to get us a bucket?" M went inside and returned with a small bucket. She said "We could only find a little one!"

December

Outside – adult supported activity

Over the weekend, all of the leaves had fallen from one of the trees. The children were helping me to sweep and collect the leaves into bin bags. M said, "What do we need to do?" I said, "we need to sweep the leaves into piles, then we need to pick them up and put them into bags." M said, "I'll hold a bag open, then I can have a turn sweeping later!" She took turns with other children, taking on the different roles independently of support.

January

Outside

Over the weekend, all of the leaves had fallen from one of the trees. While working together to sweep, them I said, "Why do we need to sweep these leaves up?" M said, "Because they look all messy! And we might slip on them!"

M had been away on holiday during half term. On return to school, she brought me a present and entered into conversation.

T: "Where did you go on holiday?" M; "I went to Menorca."
T: "How did you get there?" M: "We went to the aeroplane port." T: Who did you go with?" M: "Mummy and Daddy and J. Nani and Grandad didn't come." T: "What did you do when you were there?" M: "I had a little paddle in the sea." J went right out! Because he's big! There was a room with food in all day and you could get whatever you wanted!"

Outside – adult supported activity

The children were helping to plant daffodil bulbs. M said, "what do I have to do?" Another child said, "You have to put gloves on and dig a hole. Then you have to put the thingy in the hole." The adult said, "Yes, you have to put the bulb in the hole." M took gloves from the trolley and put them on. She then took a trowel and began to dig a hole.

UNDERSTANDING

Children can follow instructions involving several ideas or actions. They answer "how" and "why" questions about their experiences and in response to stories or events.

January

Small group, adult led activity.

The children were using Photostory programme to sequence pictures to re-tell "Peace at Last". M had "hands on the computer". Another child (B) said "click on the picture and make it go blue. Then click on the OK button." M did as B instructed to insert the picture to the Photostory.

March

Workshop – child initiated

M had made a model using a cardboard box and bottle tops. J said "Wow, M! That's good! How did you do that?" M said, "I just got the glue and put that on first. Then I just got these and put them on the top! It's a bit sticky!"

October

Outside

M was standing at the steps that lead onto the balancing equipment. K came and said, "Why are you standing there?" M replied, "Because only one at a time is allowed on. That makes it safe!" M then moved across the beam, sliding on her tummy.

May

Tidy up time

M said, "can I help?"

The adult said, "yes please...put the book in the box and tidy up the table for me."

M returned the book to the book box and began to return the story prop resources to the small world tray.

March

During the session, M and B had been using story props to re-tell the "Whatever Next" story (child initiated, following adult led activities earlier in the week). I had been observing and photographing the children as they used the props. When the children had finished, I engaged M in conversation. T: "How did Baby Bear get to the moon?" M: "In his space rocket." T: "How did he feel?" M: "Happy." T: "Why was he happy?" M: "He liked the moon." T: "Why did Mummy Bear put him in the bath?" M: "Because he was all mucky!" T: "How did he get dirty?" M: "Because he went to the moon!"

EYFS Profile exemplification Learning journey

Communication and language

ELG03 – Speaking

> **Children express themselves effectively, showing awareness of listeners' needs. They use past, present and future forms accurately when talking about events that have happened or are to happen in the future. They develop their own narratives and explanations by connecting ideas or events.**

Explanatory notes

The child uses talk to recreate, rehearse and reflect on his or her experiences and to clarify ideas and feelings. The child is keen to develop their vocabulary and may demonstrate their understanding of newly learned words by using them in context. The child speaks clearly and with confidence in both familiar and less familiar groups. They demonstrate an awareness of the listener for example by adding detail to explanations or asking questions in order to find out more information.

September

Writing area

M was drawing a picture and talking to B who was sitting beside her.

M: "I made it round for the face...and I put some feet on...and a big ear and a little ear..."

October

Outside – child initiated

M was sitting inside a tyre. As I walked by, she said "Look at me in my boat! I'm not sure where I'm going! Maybe I will go to an island, but I'm not sure yet!"

October

During the afternoon session, a child from one of the other classes came to play in M's classroom. She brought him over to me and said, "This is my new friend. We met each other this morning and then again at dinner time. We made a rocket together outside!"

During an afternoon free flow session, M and some other children were using the wii,, connected to the interactive whiteboard. M told the other children how to use the wii controller to play the bowling game. M: "Press the back button and let go...I know all about wii because my brother J has one...Now it's your go...press the back button and swing...After he's had a go he will pass it to me. Then I will pass it to her..."

M was putting pictures she had made in the workshop into her book bag.

M: "this one is the shortest, but this one is the longest. I can't fit this one into my book bag because it's too long. I don't want to bend it."

November

Outside adult supported activity (role playing a bonfire party and keeping safe)

M began collecting crates and piling them two high in a line. As she did this, she talked to other children. M: "We need to get these to make it like a fence. We will have to stand behind the fence so that we don't get burnt! Only grownups can touch the fire! It's very dangerous for children!

That's why we have to wear gloves too – so we don't get our hands burnt!"

June

During adult led activities, the children had sown and looked after grass seed, planted sunflower seeds, and had read non-fiction books about caring for plants. During an afternoon session, M noticed and commented on the classroom spider plants (which had not been part of any intentional experiments)!

M: "Look at these! They've gone all brown. We didn't look after them because we were too busy. We didn't water them."

SPEAKING

Children express themselves effectively showing awareness of listeners' needs. They use past, present and future forms accurately when talking about events that have happened or are to happen in the future. They develop their own narratives and explanations by connecting ideas or events.

November

M was talking to me as she was getting ready to go home. M: "I can't wait until I get home, because I'm only staying at home for a little bit! Me and Mummy and Daddy and J are going to get in the car and we're going all the way to my Nani's house! We will drive in the dark! And then tomorrow I think we will have some fireworks and a bonfire at Nani and Grandad's house. We have done that before. Last year I think. My granddad just lit a few fireworks in his garden and we watched them."

September

Atelier – child initiated

M was talking to another child, as she selected and arranged atelier objects on a mat.

M: "I'm making a smiley grin with some teeth...I need this for his hair (a feather)... the white ones are his teeth... these are the eyes...I need to put a nose on too!"

February

Workshop – child initiated

M was talking as she looked at the resources in the workshop area.

M: "I'm going to draw a rocket and I will cut it out...then I will stick it on my wall at home." She drew a picture, collected scissors and cut around the outline she had drawn. M: "This is my mini rocket...I'm going to write my name on the back!" She turned her rocket over and wrote her full name on the back.

EYFS Profile exemplification
Learning journey

Literacy

ELG09 – Reading

Children read and understand simple sentences. They use phonic knowledge to decode regular words and read them aloud accurately. They also read some common irregular words. They demonstrate understanding when talking with others about what they have read.

Explanatory notes

The child uses cues such as pictures, letter/word recognition, knowledge of the story or context and reading for meaning, in order to help them comprehend a range of fiction and non-fiction texts. The child blends and segments words independently and applies their phonic knowledge to regular and irregular unfamiliar words. The child shares his or her feelings and ideas about what they have read with others.

M and B were playing with the "Whatever Next!" story props. These had been used earlier in the week during adult led activities. They had then been left for children to use in their self-initiated activities. M and B told the story, acting it out with the props. M said "no, we haven't done the other bits yet...space boots on...helmet on...and then whoosh...on the moon!" when B tried to move the story on too quickly!

23rd November

The story props and prompt cards for "Whatever Next!" had been used earlier in the week during adult led activities. They had then been left available for children to use in child initiated play. M picked up the story prompt cards. She looked at one of the cards and pointed to the word printed on it. She pointed to each letter in the word and said "b-u-m-p, bump!" She looked at another card and again pointed to each letter in turn, saying "m-oo-n, moon!". She looked at a third card – "C-a-n, can I go to the m-oo-n, moon, can I go to the moon?" She repeated this sentence again, using a "Baby Bear voice".

Notes from M's parent, written in home-school link book

10th October: "M has been very proud of herself sounding out CVC words – we are very proud of her too!"

12th October: "Tonight M just wanted to look at Jolly Phonics books and build words. She has been singing your blending song too!"

31st October: "She is a star! She reads everything and anything she can – we call her a spelling machine!"

3rd November: "M's reading is just getting better and better all the time. She is so confident to have a go at reading all the words in her reading book."

5th October

Earlier in the day, "Peace at Last" had been read during an adult led shared reading session. M then chose to look at the book again during child initiated, free flow time.

M was sitting on a chair, balancing the "Peace at Last" big book against her legs. She had turned the book so that the pictures faced another child who was sitting on the floor.

M turned the pages, and re-told the story from the pictures to the other child.

M: "Drip, drop, drip drop...then he went outside...he tried to sleep in the car!"

Interactive whiteboard

During the afternoon session, M chose to use the IWB (the activity had been used earlier in the day as a whole class phonics activity). M "pressed the sound buttons" to read the CVC words, saying "b-a-g, bag...e-g-g, egg...b-a-t, bat". She then quickly matched the pictures to the words.

Book corner

M had a Jolly Phonics book open on her knee. She was talking to J.

M said "I know what all of these say: s-i-t, sit, p-a-t, pat, t-i-p, tip, p-a-n, pan". For each word, she pointed to letters in turn, left to right, saying each letter sound, then blending them together.

READING

Children read and understand simple sentences. They use phonic knowledge to decode regular words and read them aloud accurately. They also read some common irregular words. They demonstrate understanding when talking with others about what they have read.

10th June

Small world – child initiated

A selection of puppets had been left out for children to access during their child-initiated activities (a mixture of characters from Cinderella and Little Red Riding Hood). M had sorted the puppets, keeping the Red Riding Hood ones inside the tray. She moved puppets around the tray, talking to another child.

M: "Once upon a time, there was a little girl called Little Red Riding Hood...she saw the wolf...where are you going? , said the wolf...what big eyes you have! You're not my grandma...!"

30th November

During adult led sessions, the children had read and re-told "We're Going on a Bear Hunt!" using picture prompt cards and small world resources. The children had also previously been shown how to use the Photostory programme on Netbooks to sequence pictures, add voice recordings and text to re-tell stories. During session time, the Netbooks were available for children to choose to use. An adult was available to support if necessary, but M worked independently, talking to herself as she selected and clicked to add pictures: "It's the grass first...then it's the water...it's the mud...there we go...a snowstorm...and the bear".

See attachment – M's Bear Hunt Photostory

5th January

Book corner

M was sitting with another child and had a book open. She pointed to the words, blending to read some, and reading others on sight.

M – "S-a-m, sam was h-a-v-i-ng, Sam was having a n-a-p, nap. Sam was having a nap."

She turned to the other child and said "look, he's really tired!"

8th June

Book corner

M was looking at "Titch" with a friend. She pointed to the word hammer, and read "h-a-m-m-er, hammer. That's a word we used in phonics to learn the er sound." She then put the book down and began to tap the fingers of her right hand on the palm of her left hand. She began to sing "Peter taps one hammer, one hammer, Peter taps with one hammer all day long!" (a song we had learnt during music sessions to help with keeping the pulse).

EYFS Profile exemplification Learning journey

Literacy

ELG10 – Writing

> **Children use their phonic knowledge to write words in ways which match their spoken sounds. They also write some irregular common words. They write sentences which can be read by themselves and others. Some words are spelt correctly and others are phonetically plausible.**

Explanatory notes

The child writes for a range of purposes in meaningful contexts. The child's writing may include features of different forms such as stories, lists, labels, captions, recipes, instructions and letters. The child's writing is phonetically plausible when he or she writes simple regular words and particularly when he or she attempts to write more complex words. The child and others can read and make sense of the text.

28th September

Writing area – gravel trays (child initiated)

M used her right hand index finger in the gravel tray. She said "I can write the a in my name properly now. You have to go all the way round, up, down and a little flick!" As she talked through the formation, she formed the letter a correctly in the gravel.

31st October

Outside – child initiated

M said, "can I play with the chalk?" She took a piece and began to write letters. She said, "I can write my second name now." She said each of the letter sounds in turn as she wrote her name on the floor. She formed all of the letters in her second name correctly.

Interactive whiteboard – child initiated

The activity had been used during a phonics session, but had been left on the interactive whiteboard for children to access independently during the afternoon. Each screen showed a picture of a CVC object, and had a range of letters for children to drag and drop onto a phoneme frame. M looked at the first picture and said, "hat, h-a-t". She dragged each letter in order onto the frame to spell the word. She repeated this with "pig" and "cat" – orally segmenting the word before dragging and dropping the matching letters.

WRITING

Children use their phonic knowledge to write words in ways which match their spoken sounds. They also write some irregular common words. They write sentences which can be read by themselves and others. Some words are spelt correctly and others are phonetically plausible.

13th June

Writing area – child initiated

M spent most of the morning session in the writing area! She brought her writing to me and said, "This is what I did at the weekend!"

She did not have to tell me what she had written as I could read it all without mediation!

May and June

Writing area – child initiated

M was extremely excited about her new rabbit! She brought photos in to show to the class, and during this time often chose to draw pictures of her rabbit. On several occasions, she also added sentences to her pictures.

5th January

Writing area – child initiated

M brought some writing to show me. She said, "This is what I got for Christmas. I got a doll for Christmas."

3rd February

Writing area – child initiated

M was playing with two other children (B and E). M was carrying a clipboard and pen.

M: "we're playing Pizza Hut. I'm taking the order."

B: "a spicy one" M wrote spiysee. E: "chicken" M wrote chic.

E: "a hot one". M wrote hot.

B: "can I have a meat pizza?". M wrote meet.

Outside – child initiated

M picked up some chalk and began to draw. She said "I'm drawing you!" She continued to draw, then said "I can write your name – miss, m-i-ss" (she orally segmented). She wrote mis underneath her picture. She drew a second picture and said "This is Jacob. I can write Jacob. J-ai-c-u-b" (she orally segmented). She wrote JakuB under her picture. I asked if she could write anything else: I said some CVC words, M orally segmented these and wrote them with the chalk. She then also wrote" the" and "no" on the floor.

25th February

Writing area – child initiated

M was playing with B, using the Beebot – programming the toy to move and stop on picture cards. When the toy stopped, the children said words and captions to one another, and M wrote them down. This had previously been an adult led phonics activity, which had been left for children to access during their child-initiated play.

25th February

Writing area – child initiated

M returned to the classroom from her phonics group. She went into the writing area and selected paper and a pen. She said, "I can write captions and sentences!"

She appeared to "make pictures in her head", then wrote sentences to match, orally segmenting words and saying sentences to herself as she wrote them down.

5th April

Writing area – child initiated

As part of adult led activities earlier in the week, the children had looked at and investigated "spring objects", had described what they could see in "spring pictures" and had written sentences with support. Blank writing frames had been left for children to use in their child-initiated activities. M said, "I've written I can see some blossom trees growing in the grass and I can see some daisies growing."